Hey! Can You Hear Us?
Messages from Animals

Hey! Can You Hear Us?
Messages from Animals

Myra Logan

with

Lin Sharp

CRYSTALSPECTRUM
PUBLICATIONS, LLC

Asheville, North Carolina

Library of Congress Cataloging-in-Publication Data

Logan, Myra, 1949-
Hey! can you hear us? : messages from animals / Myra Logan ; with Lin Sharp.
pages cm

LCCN 2013954640

ISBN 978-0-9911532-0-6

1. Logan, Myra, 1949- 2. Animal communicators--Texas
--Biography. 3. Pet psychics--Texas--Biography.
4. Human-animal communication. 5. Telepathy--Anecdotes.
I. Sharp, Lin. II. Title.

SF411.45.L64H49 2013 133.8'2'092

QBI13-2477

Printed in the United States

A portion of all proceeds from this book goes to
animal rescue organizations

Published by

CRYSTALSPECTRUM
PUBLICATIONS, LLC
Asheville, North Carolina

www.crystalspectrumpublications.com

This book is dedicated to Trina, my beautiful and loving canine companion of many years.

TABLE OF CONTENTS

FORWARD   xi

ACKNOWLEDGMENTS   xiii

CHAPTER ONE
What Is this Crazy Animal Communication Stuff?   1
 So, Your Dog Won't Get into the Car Anymore…
 A Cinderella Story
 Third Time's a Charm

CHAPTER TWO
Jumping Off the Cliff   9
 My Story
 A Kick in the Butt
 Vision Quest
 Who Is Talking to Me?
 Blind Trust

CHAPTER THREE
An Amazing Schoolroom   17
 Straight from the Zebra's Mouth
 Desdemona, the Tarantula
 Cow Etiquette and Horse Protocol
 Twinky's Gratitude
 Babaganash and the Apple
 Bowie, the English Bulldog

CHAPTER FOUR
An Ounce of Prevention Is Worth More than a Pound of Cure 25
 From Wasted Wuss to Wonderdog
 The Sock–Eating Dog
 From Hunter to Homebody
 No Leapin' Lizards
 Unhappy Prairie Chickens
 Same Old Stuff
 A Golden Predicament
 Stormy
 Remy

CHAPTER FIVE
Behavior Changes: What's in It for Me?   **37**
    To Pee or Not to Pee
    Ollie Bubba—B&B Bully
    Camera–Shy Dog
    Last–Chance Sheltie
    Marco the Magnificent
    Mini Pin Without a Soul
    Cat Arbitration

CHAPTER SIX
Lost and Rescued Pets   **51**
    Run for Your Life
    Winnie the Pooh
    Alabama Dachshunds
    Saleem the Jester
    Diana's Dilemma
    The Kitty Connection

CHAPTER SEVEN
Deceased Pets   **61**
    Reba and RJ
    Betsy and Glory
    Buckwheat
    Java's Last Adventure
    Living Life on the Edge

CHAPTER EIGHT
Do You See What I See?   **69**
    Mandy and the Haunted House
    Rat Haunting
    The Cowboy Ghost
    Leo's Intervention
    Two Scotties
    Sadie and Libby
    Casper
    Marbi and the Mystery Music
    Persian Tale
    A Memorable Gift
    Family Reunion
    Woody's Jitters

CHAPTER NINE
The Funny Side of Animals   81
    Pets Say the Darndest Things
    Powerful Princess
    Special Requests
    Maverick
    Rabbit Reprimand

CHAPTER TEN
A Talk with the Wild Side   89
    Ants and Squirrels?
    Resistant Racoon
    Baby Bears and a Puma
    Harried Horse
    George the Fish
    Fish Fan
    Wild and Free
    Awkward Observation
    Two Crickets and a Frog Walk into the Room…

CHAPTER ELEVEN
Are You Ready to Listen?   97
    Reasons for Communication
    Receiving Information
    Initiating Contact
    Physical Preparation
    Meditation
    Suggestions for a Successful Communication
    Clearing Energy
    Animal Communication Styles

CHAPTER TWELVE
Who Is the Higher Species?   111
    Border Collie Lesson
    Slithery Stuff
    Cat–Alysts for Personal Growth
    A Head Start

CHAPTER THIRTEEN
An Awesome Ending   119
    Putting All the Chips on the Table
    A French Bulldog Love Story
    Awesome and the Girl with the Pink Shoes

FOREWORD

Myra is an ordinary person who, through a debilitating illness, chose to be healthy. Open to ideas, she was guided to a Chinese doctor who cured her. Myra had the foresight to ask the doctor to also assist in opening her third eye. Hence was the inception of a psychic career. Through exercise, meditation, yoga, books, seminars, alternative doctors, healers and life's experiences, she has honed her skills to become one of the finest intuitive pet psychics in Texas. Lucky for me, I have been along to witness the entire transformation.

I am a holistic veterinarian. In my clientele the animals are family. If things are not well with the pet, the family is truly in turmoil. I understand the enormity of this role entrusted to me to restore the health and well–being of my patient. Sometimes, no matter how thorough and conscientious I am, the blood work, physical examination and other tests performed do not identify the problem. There is no place for ego here. I must be open to all modalities, conventional and unconventional, to find the answers to facilitate a cure.

What a blessing to be able to call on Myra to help discover the missing piece of the puzzle needed to solve a difficult and unresponsive case, to identify a vague complaint, and to get to the bottom of a behavioral issue that has mystified me and the trainer.

What a joy it is to share Myra with my clients and their animals. Initial skepticism gives way to a new, much deeper understanding of their pets. They are privileged to a glimpse into the bigger picture of their relationship with profound messages and lessons to be learned. It is truly life changing. I am witness to the exponential growth of love and respect in their human and animal bond.

As a veterinarian, the toughest thing I face is end of life. I am part of the extended family and heartbroken as well. Myra's ability to communicate the animals' wishes to the humans during transition is a godsend. This helps to lessen the miserable burden of guilt the family and veterinarian are bearing. The room lights up as pets, friends, and family members that have passed gather among us to receive the transitioning pet or to comfort those of us left behind. Myra gives us a detailed account of the goings–on to erase any doubt. Incredibly, Myra softens the initial morbid atmosphere into one of wonder and amazement. Now euthanasia becomes a celebration of life.

Working with Myra has made my practice anything but boring. I cherish her wisdom, her insight, her humor, her friendship and for her giving me that edge in solving the mysteries in my profession. Myra and I strive to better the lives of people and animals, and it is truly enlightening when we work together.

Happy Babbish, DVM
Houston, Texas

ACKNOWLEDGMENTS

This collection of stories about my actual experiences in animal communications spans more than a decade. Names have been changed and details minimized to protect the privacy of my clients.

Many of the stories are short anecdotes because I prefer to approach each case in an objective manner with very little background knowledge regarding the animals and people. Most animals communicate in a very to–the–point style, and they may not offer a complete story. The particular information I receive is sufficient to provide assistance to the humans and the animals. I may never learn about the long–term results from some of the sessions. Occasionally, clients or other people provide follow–up information. This book includes the most relevant material to illustrate the point of each story.

My success has been, and continues to be, mentored by outstanding souls. Happy Babbish, an extraordinary veterinarian and my best friend, encouraged me to seek alternative treatments for a serious illness. Her advice led me to Yang Research Center where my illness was cured and my intuitive abilities were released. Holistic health practitioners Dr. Otis Thomas, Jamey Summerfield, and Dr. Susan Moss aided me in maintaining my health. Their mentoring also increased my intuitive abilities.

Friends and clients sustained me by providing encouragement, honest feedback, and referrals. Nikki Patillo, an author of several spiritual books, gave me publishing advice and inspired me. And I don't know how I could have made it through the transition into my current career without the friendship and loyalty of Karen Senft. Sherry Petraitis, Patrice Charleville, Candace Wingo, Crista Meyer, and Sita Hood have supported me through my various growth stages. I am so grateful to Clair Amonett for her graciousness to me and my clients at her pet boutique. Renee Harkey introduced me to contacts that resulted in fun and outlandish experiences that were important to my psychic education.

Although I never planned to write a book, I received a very strong inner push from my guides and angels to share my experiences. A string of synchronistic events moved me forward in this endeavor. At one point, I felt overwhelmed with the enormity of the task, so I put out a clear request to the universe for help in organizing and writing down material I had collected. A few days later, during a scheduled speaking event, I shared my animal communication experiences with the membership of a large local group. Afterward, a woman approached me and said, "You need to write a book." This initiated an important business partnership, then deep friendship with entrepreneur, writer, and publisher, Lin Sharp.

ACKNOWLEDGMENTS

I am especially grateful to the animals, domestic and wild, who have contributed the majority of the information in this book. They taught me my most significant lessons by allowing me to see the world through their point of view. As I groped to understand the challenges they presented to me, I appreciated their patience, grace, and humor.

Most of all, I am indebted to Trina, my beloved canine companion who completed her soul partnership with me and passed away before this book was published. Trina loped along beside me as my running buddy when I began exercising as part of my physical recovery. Because she attracted humans and animals with her elegant and gentle demeanor, I considered her my business partner. She still connects with me in spirit to offer explanations and advice.

Finally, my intention in writing this book is to enhance human/animal relationships by encouraging understanding and love.

With gratitude,

Myra Logan
Montgomery, Texas

CHAPTER ONE

What is This Crazy Animal Communication Stuff?

"Give me the gift of a listening heart."

~*King Solomon*

SO, YOUR DOG WON'T GET INTO THE CAR ANYMORE . . .

Suddenly, your dog refuses to get into the car. What do you do?

This was Bobbie's dilemma. Bobbie had acquired a new best friend, a black designer dog called a Charlie Bear. Her Charlie Bear is the hybrid result of breeding a Portuguese water dog and a soft coated wheaton terrier. Bobbie enjoyed the nine–month–old puppy, Gracie, so much that Gracie became her constant companion. Gracie rode in the front seat of the car right next to Bobbie as they rode around town on short errands. Without warning, Gracie became terrified of the car. When Bobbie tried to coax her onto the seat, the puppy would balk and pull back for no apparent reason. Gracie absolutely refused to enter the vehicle.

Bobbie hired a top–rated Houston dog trainer to help her overcome Gracie's resistant behavior. When he couldn't persuade Gracie to get into the car, Bobbie consulted her veterinarian. None of the tests the veterinarian administered indicated any medical problem associated with Gracie's behavior. The vet suggested that Bobbie contact me. Bobbie expressed her skepticism about using an animal communicator, but the veterinarian assured Bobbie she had witnessed many positive results coming from my consultations, particularly with animal behavior. Bobbie agreed to a session as a last resort.

I traveled to Bobbie's home to talk with Gracie and discover how I could be of help. When I asked Gracie why she wouldn't get in the car, Gracie complained that she was so fearful when she rode in the car, that she actually felt sick. She said Bobbie shopped a lot and would fill up the seat and set all the scary shopping bags between them. When I delivered this information to Bobbie, she hesitated in responding to Gracie's remarks. However, her daughter Kristi, who was also listening to my explanation, immediately confirmed the dog's comments about her mother's shopping habits.

At that moment, I sensed an additional energy in the room—male and strongly connected to Bobbie. The energy identified himself as Bobbie's husband and let me know he had passed away the previous year. He insisted on interjecting his comments concerning Gracie's problem.

He said to me point–blank, "That dog is scared because Bobbie drives like a bat out of hell!"

His interruption and presence created a dilemma for me. How could I communicate this information tactfully to

Bobbie? She was already uncomfortable about my ability to communicate with her dog. Now I was communicating with her dead husband!

I gathered up my courage and repeated her husband's wisecrack. Her jaw dropped wide open.

"I guess he knows about my speeding ticket."

At the conclusion of the session, I suggested she make the car more comfortable and less frightening by stowing the shopping bags in the trunk and slowing down when she drives. She could let Gracie ride in the back seat to increase her feeling of security. With patience, practice, and using what I discovered was Gracie's favorite treat, bits of roast beef, Bobbie eventually enticed her into the car. Bobbie was very pleased that Gracie could travel with her once again.

A CINDERELLA STORY

Like so many unwanted cats, Lulu's future looked bleak. Her previous caretakers had adopted her from a shelter and later decided she complicated their lifestyle. A veterinary clinic in one of the poorest areas of Houston agreed to try to place her into a good home with one of their clients. In the meantime, they confined Lulu to a small cage where she waited patiently for a new place to live. After ten long months with no prospective home in sight, the clinic decided she would have to be euthanized.

My friend and holistic veterinarian, Dr. Happy Babbish, met the beautiful tortoiseshell cat during a weekend veterinarian rotation at the clinic. Her compassion for Lulu's plight led her to approach a friend, Mike, and ask him to at least meet Lulu. She hoped Lulu could fill a void in Mike's life, created by the recent passing of his previous cat, one that he had loved and pampered for many years. Mike finally agreed to meet Lulu at his home and introduce her to his wife.

Dr. Babbish called me to prepare Lulu for the intense inspection she was about to receive before the arranged meeting. It was imperative that Lulu create a positive first impression with Mike and his wife, because her alternative was certain death.

Mike and his wife held misgivings about adopting another cat. They had just purchased an expensive sofa and wanted to protect the fabric from destructive scratching. Dr. Babbish advises her clients not to have cats' claws removed, because it causes intense pain and continued debilitating consequences. It would be mandatory that Lulu confine her clawing to the scratching posts and pads that would be made available to her.

A second hurdle in securing Lulu's new home was Mike's wife's intense fear of cats. Lulu needed to immediately ingratiate herself to Mike's wife because his previous cat had attacked her several times. That aggressive behavior had only increased her tension around cats. Finally, Lulu needed to understand that this was her only opportunity for a good life in a loving home. She would have to act perfectly charming!

When I communicated all this information to Lulu, I received a response of dead silence. I knew this intelligent cat had received my information, so I decided to give her a little more time to digest it completely. The next morning I connected with her again, just to make certain she understood what was expected of her and how critical this test would be. As I began to repeat the instructions, she suddenly interrupted me.

"I got it the first time!" she said in a matter–of–fact tone.

"Great, and good luck!" was my surprised response.

Dr. Babbish took Lulu to Mike's home for her conditional inspection that same afternoon. Lulu left the crate and strode directly to Mike's wife. She rubbed up against her legs begging to be stroked. Then Mike selected one of Lulu's cat toys and tossed it across the room. Lulu looked up at Dr. Babbish as if to say, "Should I play with it?"

Dr. Babbish mentally assured her it was OK, so Lulu chased the toy.

Lulu passed her test. The couple fell in love with her.

THIRD TIME'S A CHARM

Ms. Matthew purchased a three–year–old champion thoroughbred mare for her young granddaughter to train for Western Pleasure competition. Soon afterward, the Red Roan Tobiano exhibited signs of discomfort and could not perform. An equestrian vet clinic examined Camille, but found no medical issues. Ms. Matthew's friend referred her to me with the hope that I could identify the problem as either behavioral or medical. I connected with the horse in a telephone session. She sent me a strong mental picture of a fracture in her right front leg as the source of her discomfort. After the consultation, Ms. Matthew relayed the information to her veterinarian. He disagreed with the assessment because he had not found any indication of a fracture during his exam.

I was surprised when Ms. Matthew called me for a second reading on the same issue. The first connection had been very convincing to me, but I agreed to the second reading because I was fairly new to animal communication at that time and wanted to test my abilities. The information provided by the mare was exactly the same—the horse had sustained a fracture in the right front leg. Ms. Matthew contacted her vet once again and received the same response.

Ms. Matthew feared we had missed some important detail. She convinced me to conduct a final session that yielded the same results. She then insisted that the vet run more extensive tests. The new tests verified a fracture in the right front leg and the mare finally received the proper treatment for her injury. She eventually healed and returned to competition.

The three cases described above illustrate some of the benefits of animal communication. Bobbie was able to modify her own behavior in a way that created a more trusting bond with her pet once she understood the source of her puppy's fear. And Gracie opened the door for Bobbie to connect with her husband. In Lulu's situation, the human coaching gave her an opportunity to choose a new and better life. The direct consultation with Camille resulted in a correct diagnosis and subsequent proper medical treatment. Although these are simple stories, they point to larger truths. Clearly, discourse between human and animal species offers an opportunity for us to enhance the quality of each other's lives.

Animal communication encompasses more than just moderating behavior, saving an animal from euthanasia, or treating a medical problem. It is a dialogue between souls that opens our world to a potential of experience beyond anything we could have previously imagined. The more we increase our overall awareness through interspecies communication, the more we increase our possibilities in life and what it means to exist as a soul in a human body or a soul in an animal body. When we observe the universe through an animal's senses like the shamans of indigenous cultures, remarkable information emerges that so enlarges our worldview, we become forever changed.

CHAPTER TWO

Jumping Off the Cliff

"We are not human beings on a spiritual journey. We are spiritual beings on a human journey."

~ *Stephen R. Covey*

MY STORY

I am often asked, "What led you to become an animal communicator?" It makes me laugh because I understand the astonishment behind the question. No one plans on being a pet psychic when they grow up. Who would have ever thought my profession would be a legitimate career? Surely not me! I had been working in a big–city corporate environment for thirty–five years. In my last conventional job, I served as Assistant to the Senior Vice President and General Counsel of a major energy company. Office work, vacations, and shopping comprised my world.

A KICK IN THE BUTT

All that changed for me in 1997, when I developed a serious illness. A sudden onset of hearing loss, accompanied by constant vertigo, interfered with my ability to function. Simple daily activities such as brushing my teeth, watching television, and walking became demanding and difficult chores. My concern about my deteriorating health increased. I decided to consult a medical specialist.

He performed a battery of tests on me and asked countless questions. His test results confirmed my vertigo and revealed a ninety percent loss of my hearing. He diagnosed my condition as Meniere's disease, a chronic disorder of the inner ear that matched my symptoms of hearing loss and severe vertigo. I was sent home with a collection of prescriptions to lessen my discomfort. After doing extensive research, I discovered there is no cure for Meniere's disease, only various (and mostly unsuccessful) attempts to control the symptoms with medication. I opted to take the drugs with the least number of side effects and just tough it out, a strategy that always seemed to work for me in the past.

In spite of the medication, my illness continued to escalate to the point where I could no longer hide the symptoms from my co–workers. Drop attacks caused my legs to buckle, and I would fall down and vomit for hours. Several times a week my co–workers drove me home from work. I feared I would lose my job and soon be headed for a wheelchair and a nursing home.

For months, my veterinarian friend, Dr. Babbish, had been urging me to visit a Chinese doctor who cured patients' maladies with an innovative energy therapy. I was so desperate for relief I decided to schedule an appointment even though I was doubtful that this unfamiliar treatment could actually help me. To my complete amazement, I felt better after the first treatment. I committed to daily treatments. Each week, my lessening symptoms encouraged me to continue the regimen. My co–workers teased me about the "voodoo treatments" as they commented on my improved health.

The Meniere's disease disappeared after four months of the energy therapy, and I experienced unexpected and additional benefits. Some intuitive abilities, suppressed since childhood, were restored. This inspired me to take classes in meditation and psychic development to further enhance my intuition.

VISION QUEST

My 50th birthday approached in late November 1999. I felt drawn to celebrate with a visit to Sedona and northern Arizona, a trip that would function as a type of vision quest to sort out questions about my life purpose. My trip plan included standing on the South Rim of the Grand Canyon at sunrise on the morning of my birthday. The trip promised to be more enjoyable when my friend Karen decided to accompany me.

We stopped in Phoenix to visit another friend when we first arrived in Arizona. The beautiful desert sky and scenery around her backyard pool inspired us to take some photographs that later proved significant to me.

In the morning we headed north to the next destination on our magical journey—the Grand Canyon. The hiking and spectacular scenery set the stage for a delightful trip. We especially enjoyed the stories the park rangers told us about all the electrical and magnetic vortices in the Canyon. On my birthday at sunrise, we stood on the South Rim for barely five minutes. Ten degrees Fahrenheit was too cold for two women from subtropical Houston to tolerate for more than a few minutes. We raced inside for a big hearty breakfast and some heat in the nearby lodge.

We moved on to our next stop and arrived in Sedona the day before Thanksgiving. It felt like home! Everything seemed right even though the town was unusually deserted. A string of coincidences led us to seek out a guided jeep tour, and we were thrilled when the woman at the reservations desk assured us we could sign up for a tour on Thanksgiving Day.

Due to the holiday, Karen and I waited at the tour office the next morning as the only customers. A tall handsome man approached us and introduced himself as our guide. His unique qualifications made him an ideal choice to lead us through our personal explorations. He had abandoned a career as a successful investment banker in New York to travel the world and study with shamans. His interest in Native American shamanism had landed him in Sedona.

"Do you have any specific requests for our itinerary today?" he asked.

I immediately blurted out, "I'm on a spiritual quest. Could a guided meditation be part of our tour?"

"Sure. I can help you discover your spirit guides."

This tour and perfect day exceeded my expectations. The sun shone through a bright blue sky as we breathed in the crisp clean air of the high desert. We sat on the bank by the clear running water of Oak Creek, while our guide played haunting melodies on the flute and told us legends about the spirits in the water. We hiked up a winding trail to sacred Indian ground. Then we sat down on the big red rocks and quieted ourselves in preparation for a half–hour meditation.

Our guide instructed us to close our eyes and visualize a tube of bright light coming down from the sky. He suggested we place the damaged parts of our bodies into the light for healing.

I thought to myself, *Well, I'm just going to fix everything*, so I placed my entire body into the tube of light.

As the meditation continued, we invited our animal spirit guides to reveal themselves to us. In my mind's eye, I immediately saw a big black bird standing right next to me. I could feel its physical presence. Soon more black birds flew all around us. I could hear them and feel the air on my body from their flapping wings. Ignoring the urge to open my eyes, I thought to myself, *what is all this about*?

At the end of the meditation, we reviewed our experiences. I told our guide I had jumped into the light with my entire body. He laughed and said, "Nobody's ever done that before!" When he prompted us to describe our animal spirit guides, Karen said, "I saw a really beautiful white horse."

As she was talking about the horse I thought to myself, *Oh great, she's got the beautiful white horse and I've got the big ugly black bird*. I heard a voice inside me say, "Myra, this means something," so I thought, *OK* and listened. When Karen finished her description, our guide said it meant she had built up spiritual energy, but she hadn't done anything with it. I remembered thinking, that's true about her.

❖ 13 ❖

And then he turned to me and asked, "What did you see?"

"I saw a big black bird."

That remark excited Karen. She jumped in, "Did you hear and feel all those birds around us during the meditation?" She had sensed the birds too, and so had our guide.

He told me, "Your spirit guide is the raven. That is typically the spirit guide of especially psychic people."

Karen added that I was, indeed, psychic. This experience with our guide and the meditation confirmed to me that I was heading in the right direction by developing my psychic skills. I left Sedona feeling successful in my quest to receive answers.

When I returned home to Houston, I developed my photos, among them the lovely photos by the pool in Phoenix. Those photos were light–smudged, and I thought the camera had malfunctioned. A friend looked at them and recognized the smudges as radiant light all around me. In that moment, I knew my spiritual guides had been present to share their encouragement and support. The pictures proved to be my second confirmation.

WHO IS TALKING TO ME?

Two years later, I sat at a table in a busy outdoor café with a close friend, Seth, and his co–workers. They wanted to meet me to explore the possibility of a personal psychic reading. As I was enjoying my lunch, I was surprised to hear a male cat talking to me. There were no cats visible in the restaurant. I felt a connection between this cat and the woman sitting across from me. "Do you have a male cat?" I asked.

"Yes. He's an orange tabby."

"He is telling me that you bought him some new toys but didn't give them to him. He wants to know why."

"Well, his birthday isn't until next week, so I wrapped his presents and hid them in the closet."

"He is saying he wants the one with the purple feather, and he wants it now!"

Seth leaned over the table and asked her, "Did you buy one with a purple feather?"

She replied with obvious astonishment, "Yes, I did."

This first experience of animal communication opened the door to an abundance of new clients. Wonderful conversations with a great variety of species gave me insights into animal behavior, motivations, and social protocol. With every experience I learned something new.

BLIND TRUST

As word of my ability spread, I found myself working a second job. Readings were so enjoyable that I considered transitioning into the intuitive consulting business full–time. I felt a desire to be of better service to others, and I knew I would be able to offer helpful information that could improve their lives. This idea placed me in a quandary, as I would have to relinquish a well–paying position with good benefits.

Four years after my first visit with the Chinese doctor, I found myself less enthusiastic about my daytime corporate job and more excited about my second vocation. Still, every time I was about to jump off the cliff and devote myself fully to a somewhat controversial career, fear would overcome me. I questioned my ability to fully support myself. After all, I was accustomed to a steady paycheck.

This tug–of–war between work interests continued for another year. It finally occurred to me to ask my guides and angels for assistance. They had always been with me, but I hadn't really acknowledged their presence until I became more spiritually developed. Once I turned my decision over to them, everything fell into place. The idea of trusting in a higher power is easy, but putting that trust into practice is sometimes difficult. It took all my courage to allow future events to unfold. The universe will support us if we just get out of the way. The leap in 2002 from the security of my corporate job into a life of daily adventure surprised me with a supportive landing.

CHAPTER THREE

An Amazing Schoolroom

"The purpose of education is to replace an empty mind with an open one."

~ *Malcolm Forbes*

The lessons I receive from my incredible creature clients in this schoolroom called Earth surpass any curriculum I could possibly imagine. I've learned not to make any assumptions during a reading, because the information that emerges constantly astounds me. I've also learned that most humans remain at preschool level when it comes to understanding other species.

STRAIGHT FROM THE ZEBRA'S MOUTH

Years ago I decided to test my new abilities as an animal communicator at a local zoo. As I approached the zebra pen, a male zebra made eye contact with me and came running to the fence. I thought, *Oh, this is going to be interesting*. I introduced myself and then asked him, "Is there anything I can do for you?"

Immediately, I received a picture in my head of a herd of zebra passing by an acacia tree at sunset in the Serengeti. The meaning he conveyed with his picture was, "Get me out of here. I want to go home." This message confused me, as I knew this zebra had been born in captivity, and I wondered how he could know anything about Africa. He told me that knowledge of his species was built into his DNA. I surmised that he held a cellular memory from which he could access his ancestry. What a surprise!

I felt very sorry that I could not help him with his request and let him know that I didn't have the authority to move him. I apologized to him and also told him he was performing a valuable service to humans by educating us about zebras. Feeling like I had to do something else positive for him, I asked if he would like me to request a favorite food for him from his keeper.

He quickly replied, "Well yes. I haven't had carrots for a while."

Suddenly, I realized what I had done. Now I had to go find the zookeeper and explain that I had just been talking to the zebra! I knew it was important to follow through on a request to foster the animal's trust. An unkept promise shows up in a human's energy field and has consequences. In my case, if I did not follow through, future animal communications would be tainted because they would be aware of my untrustworthiness. I can only hope that zebra's custodian fulfilled the request. Since then, I have learned to be more careful in my communications with animals.

DESDEMONA, THE TARANTULA

Desdemona's caretaker, Lana, worked as a vet tech at an animal clinic that frequently requested my services. Lana suspected that Desdemona was unhappy. When she showed me Desdemona's photo, I was able to connect. Her observation was correct. The tarantula was very unhappy. Lana had rescued her from a failing pet store and had placed her in an aquarium, a habitat that made Desdemona uncomfortable. I asked how Lana could make her feel more at ease. She told me it was vital for her to connect with the soil and the earth's magnetic force.

Lana agreed to let her "play in the dirt" whenever possible. She constructed an enclosure that kept Desdemona contained but allowed her to touch the ground. Desdemona also requested a volcanic rock be placed in her aquarium, a desire that Lana cheerfully fulfilled. Lana later told me that Desdemona rarely moved from her rock perch and really seemed to enjoy her outings in her new playground.

COW ETIQUETTE AND HORSE PROTOCOL

I committed two major animal faux pas early in my career. I had approached a herd of cows in a friend's pasture as it neared lunchtime. For some reason a picture of a big juicy hamburger, my favorite food, just popped into my head. All the cows in the herd raised their heads simultaneously, looked at me, and then ran in the opposite direction. I was stunned! I apologized immediately and told them that, since they were my friend's pets, they were perfectly safe. But they would have nothing to do with me after that. This experience taught me that animals clearly possess telepathic abilities.

The second incident happened during a consultation with four horses. My client had listed her questions in the order of importance, addressing issues with the three geldings first and then the mare. After I spoke with the three geldings, I initiated contact with the mare.

She stated flatly, "I'm not talking to you because you talked to the geldings first."

Abashed, I realized I had violated some kind of horse protocol. I apologized and told her it would never happen again. The client agreed to schedule another consultation with the mare at a later date. Since then, I have learned to let the animals guide me through the acceptable order of their social hierarchy.

TWINKY'S GRATITUDE

Most people will acknowledge that their pets express emotion. Twinky's account brought me to tears. A beautiful Palomino horse, Twinky sent me a mental image of an arena. I intuitively knew this arena was a horse auction. She expressed tremendous gratitude to her new caretakers, for they had just saved her from a dog food company. When I relayed this information, her caretakers confirmed that they had purchased her at an auction attended by dog food companies actively bidding on the horses. Twinky's intense emotion and her keen awareness regarding that situation bolstered my knowledge of animal cognition.

BABAGANASH AND THE APPLE

Ann wanted to avoid past issues with her pregnant mare, Babaganash. During a phone session with Babaganash,

I learned that information I often receive in symbolic form can have multiple meanings. Before we finished, Babaganash telepathically sent me a picture of a red apple with the feeling of desire to have one. I passed the information on to Ann and asked her to send me feedback. Later, I received the following email:

> After speaking with you last week, I bought Babaganash the red apples she had requested. I was so looking forward to seeing her joy at getting what she wanted. She sniffed the apple, and then gave me the "You are a stupid human" look. OK, Babs. I sliced the apples, and still no interest! I peeled the apples. No. Hmmm.
>
> Then, the rains came, and all the horses were put in the barn in their appropriate stalls. This is when I realized that most of the horses have a toy hanging in their stalls that is—yes, you guessed it—a big bright red apple. Now, Baba-g already had a red apple toy in her stall, so I wasn't sure where this was going to lead. I bought her a new one, and hung it on her gate (now she has two and all others have only one.) Once she had the new toy, she licked it, she rubbed it, she balanced it on her head, and she played and played and played with it. She is a happy girl!

The red apple Babaganash wanted was not the food variety as I had assumed. She wanted a duplicate of the toy apple that hung in the stall. I had no knowledge of the toy since the reading was conducted over the telephone, not on location. During readings, the animal doesn't always include every little detail. Sometimes I have to rely on the caretaker to get an exact meaning of the information I receive and how it relates to the animal.

BOWIE, THE ENGLISH BULLDOG

Animals are aware of much more than we imagine. Bowie, an English bulldog, showed me a famous painting of bulldogs playing poker and smoking cigars. He also showed me a picture of his human "Dad" working cross-word puzzles and drinking a red drink with ice. It didn't make sense at first to Lucia, his female caretaker, but then she remembered her husband had spent time at his best friend's house a few days earlier. His friend had set up a new screensaver on his computer of, you guessed it, several bulldogs playing poker. The two men had also solved some crossword puzzles together. In addition, Dad remembered a red drink with ice he consumed that same day.

Bowie did not accompany his dad to the friend's home. How did he know what transpired that day? I learned that animals can connect to us when we are absent. They can check on us whenever they wish, even if we are on the other side of the planet.

Thanks to these animals, my general comprehension concerning their capabilities expanded. I learned they hold an ancestral memory. They are connected to the energy of the earth. They maintain a species social protocol. Many are capable of strong emotion. And, finally, they exhibit extra-sensory perception and telepathic ability.

I am confronted with situations every day that surprise me and totally change my earlier assumptions about the way the universe carries on its business. How would our world be enhanced if we all tapped into the wisdom of the animals? How might we change ourselves?

That is my purpose in writing this book—to share some of the information I have learned. My hope is that others will open themselves to greater possibilities and expand their capabilities. If you learn to communicate with an animal, you may open the door to a new life coach.

CHAPTER FOUR

An Ounce of Prevention is Worth More than a Pound of Cure

"Health is not simply the absence of sickness."

~ *Hannah Green*

FROM WASTED WUSS TO WONDERDOG

In the mid–nineties, before I communicated with animals, an experience with my own pet introduced me to the importance of proper pet nutrition. My canine companion at the time was Fluffy, an aging but beautiful white American Eskimo. As a conscientious pet owner, I had strictly followed the advice of conventional veterinarians by purchasing their recommended high–quality pet food brands. I was so strict with Fluffy's diet that my family members joked about "the Nazi dog mom" as they sneaked her pieces of turkey under the table at Thanksgiving. Looking back, I now understand some of Fluffy's puzzling behavior. For instance, she would totally ignore her dry kibble until bedtime. Then she would grudgingly gobble it up knowing she would be given absolutely nothing else to eat that day.

For five years Fluffy appeared to be in good health. Then she suddenly developed grand mal seizures. One night, I woke up to the sound of thumping. When my eyes adjusted to the room's darkness, I could see Fluffy violently banging her head against the baseboard in my bedroom. Several minutes later, the seizure abated but her eyes remained glassy. She tried to stand up and walk. Then she stumbled and ran into the furniture.

A conventional vet diagnosed Fluffy with canine epilepsy and prescribed phenobarbital as a method to control the disorder. The medication worked for a few weeks but the seizures returned with increased intensity. The vet raised the dosage with each escalation of the seizures. He monitored Fluffy's liver function constantly, as phenobarbital can cause scarring of the liver and lead to liver failure. This possibility added to my distress about her deteriorating condition. She became increasingly catatonic, a side effect of the medication. Fluffy completely lost her engaging personality.

I grew more alarmed by the changes and feared I would lose my best friend. I decided to consult a second vet, and then a third, for other opinions. They both agreed with the first vet and offered no additional solutions, except euthanasia. One day, shopping in a local health food store, I noticed a posted ad for a vet practicing holistic veterinary medicine. I immediately made an appointment for an office visit where I filled out pages of information concerning Fluffy's condition and medical history. The vet impressed me by spending two hours documenting all the minute details of Fluffy's medical history.

"Do you know what is wrong with her?" I finally asked him. "Can you cure her?"

He looked directly at me. "I know exactly what is wrong with her, and she doesn't have epilepsy. Her seizures are caused by her diet of commercial pet food." He explained that most commercial pet foods contain little nutrition and actually harm pets.

He recommended the immediate discontinuation of the medication, because her health problems were far too advanced to weather gradual withdrawal. He warned that discontinuing the medication would probably cause severe seizures and she could possibly die.

I consented to the treatment in spite of the risk.

"She's dying anyway. I know the phenobarbital is affecting her liver, so we might as well try this treatment."

The vet immediately flushed Fluffy's body using IV therapy to remove the toxins from her system. My poor baby suffered through twelve seizures that first day. She endured IV flushing for four more days and simultaneously the vet changed her diet to a home–cooked recipe. This wonderful man's treatment resulted in a gradual abatement of her seizures within the week. She completely recovered.

Fluffy's personality returned with a bonus. She had always loved people; but, as she had gotten older, she had become increasingly aggressive with other dogs. I could not take her anywhere, because she would growl and attack them. But the longer she ate the new food, the more relaxed she became in the company of other animals.

The vet explained her behavior change as a consequence of eliminating the commercial food from her diet. "That food irritates the gall bladder and encourages behavioral problems." He laughed and told me an old folk story about the phrase "she's got a lot of gall." Bile would back up in the gall bladder of women as they aged and, as a result, they became cranky. Apparently Fluffy had a lot of gall too! Fluffy not only recovered her health with her new diet—she prospered, until she passed away at the mature age of eighteen.

Fluffy's ordeal opened my awareness to the world of holistic medicine for animals. This vet's experience encompassed fifty years of veterinary medicine. Over the years he had increased his knowledge and application of alternative practices, such as administering herbal and homeopathic medicines. His own groundbreaking treatments eventually attracted veterinarians from all over the world to study with him.

Since then, the diets for animals recommended by holistic vets continue to evolve. There is no "one size fits all" when it comes to pet nutrition. It takes some experimentation to discover the perfect diet for your particular animal. So many people rely on processed pet food. However, the pet food industry as a whole is not well regulated. I encourage clients to seek advice from a holistic vet or consultant who has studied holistic pet nutrition.

In 1997, I adopted Trina, an eight–month–old Borzoi/Border Collie mix. Her previous diet of typical dry kibble had produced a bad skin irritation of large dry itchy sores, so I changed her diet. Trina's skin healed, and a shine came into her eyes and fur after ten months of eating fresh raw unprocessed food. I thank Fluffy for introducing me to a holistic method of animal care that ultimately benefited my pets, as well as many of my animal clients.

The subject of pet nutrition surfaces constantly in my readings. My first incident of a similar condition to Fluffy's dietary problems came from a reading for a veterinary clinic that often requested my assistance in communicating with its clients' animals. A white Bichon with seizures had been brought in, and by that time, my skills had advanced so I could ask her directly what bothered her. She showed me an inflamed gall bladder from the food she was given and how it made her spit up yellow liquid. When I asked the owner if the dog vomited yellow bile, she replied, "Yes." A switch to a healthier diet eliminated the dog's seizures.

THE SOCK-EATING DOG

In another case, a client called me to find out why her young dog insisted on eating her toddler's socks. This peculiar behavior had already resulted in two surgeries. The puppy told me she felt hungry all the time. She was not getting the nutrition she needed. She felt compelled to chew on something and fill the emptiness in her stomach. I suggested a switch from dry kibble to the raw diet and raw bones as a corrective measure. My client told me later that the diet completely changed her dog's behavior. Apparently raw bones taste much yummier than toddler's socks.

Dogs tell me that chewing on raw bones massages their gums and evokes feelings of security and complete relaxation. It's like the "ah" feeling after a full body massage. Raw bones act as an important tool in relieving anxiety behavior. I must emphasize that animals should chew *raw* bones, not cooked bones. Heat causes bones to become brittle. Brittle bones can splinter and cause damage in an animal's intestinal tract. Raw bones function as a natural toothbrush to decrease tarter buildup on canine teeth. Finally, dogs benefit from the nutrients in the raw bone marrow.

FROM HUNTER TO HOMEBODY

Woody's voracious appetite for hunting bothered Patrice and Sherry. This handsome orange striped tabby would return home, after frequent long absences, and proudly present his catch (sometimes still alive). His continual presentation of victims and his roaming increasingly distressed the women. They had endured the disappearance of two previous cats with a similar behavior pattern.

Woody told me he was hunting because he was hungry, so I recommended that his food be switched from dry kibble to a mostly raw diet. Patrice and Sherry told me his behavior changed dramatically after only two weeks on the new diet. He stayed closer to home and rarely brought in additional food.

The primitive hunter in Woody immediately returned when, for a short period, Patrice and Sherry reverted to his previous diet. They wasted no time in re–establishing the holistic raw, and were amazed to see their lovable and friendly homebody return.

NO LEAPIN' LIZARDS

Wholesome food is not only prescribed for domesticated animals such as dogs and cats, but also for other species as well. An example comes from a local pet store owner who occasionally retained me to talk with store animals about their various issues. The owner had acquired some exotic and expensive lizards from South America. Although she had dutifully fed them their typical diet of fruit, vegetables, and live crickets, they had stopped eating and were dying. She moved them to a back room while she searched for a remedy.

I was shocked to see live crickets hopping all around the listless lizards as I approached their habitats. "What's wrong? How can I help you, and why are you dying?" I asked.

The lizards told me that the fruits and vegetables they had been eating were covered with toxic pesticides. I advised the owner to switch to organic produce. She followed my suggestion, and the majority of the lizards soon recovered.

UNHAPPY PRAIRIE CHICKENS

A zookeeper enlisted my help in identifying some problems with some endangered prairie chickens in a private breeding program at a local zoo. Her favorite male had stopped eating. When I asked him why he had stopped eating, he sent me a visual picture of a metal storage container full of what looked like dry processed food. A white powdery substance lay in a ring around the food near the top of the container.

I asked him, "Is the white substance making you sick?"

He answered, "Yes, and that is also why we are not breeding."

I gave the information to his zookeeper and she said, "I noticed the powder and I wondered if it was related to their illness."

Nature provides perfect food sources in a species' native habitat. In the wild, these chickens live in a prairie environment abundant with insects, seeds, and leaves. The zoo chickens were held in temporary housing pending a permanent move. No insects, seeds, or leaves were available to them. Later I discovered the prairie chickens were moved to a more natural environment and this endangered species began breeding again. I never received additional information regarding the composition of the white powder.

SAME OLD STUFF

Sometimes our pets want to choose their own food. A young Brittany spaniel, Gus, certainly knew what he liked. Gus heartily enjoyed the raw food diet that replaced his commercial dry food, but months later he suddenly stopped eating it.

When I spoke with Gus, he kept repeating, "I want more variety."

I proposed that his owners try giving him duck for a change. We were confounded when Gus wouldn't eat the duck. Then, on a weekend trip to their vacation home, Gus's owners opened the freezer and discovered a bag of Nature's Variety Instinct, a holistic brand of raw dog food. Gus devoured it! When Gus said he wanted more Variety, he meant it—literally. Like people, pets usually prefer an assortment of foods for superior health and happiness.

NONTRADITIONAL THERAPIES

Many pets respond well to alternative types of therapy. When my clients have tried acupuncture, chiropractic treatments, hands–on energy healing, Chinese herbs, and natural supplements, the health of their pets improved considerably. The pets completely recovered in most cases. Acupuncture treats illnesses through the insertion of tiny sterilized needles at specific meridian (energy) points thus removing energy blockages. The removal of blockages allows the pet's energy to flow freely and increase healing. Chiropractic treatment promotes healing by manipulation of body structures. Both Chinese herbs and natural supplements address nutritional deficiencies.

Hands–on energy healing by successful healers is often overlooked as a method of health remediation for pets. People sometimes have preconceived notions that healers are scam artists. Some are actually quite skilled. I recommend asking for referrals to find legitimate healers.

A GOLDEN PREDICAMENT

A woman trained golden retrievers for agility competitions with great success, except for one dog. This dog balked at the weave poles and actually bit her at one point. The trainer called for a session and told me she just couldn't work with this particular dog. I sensed that the dog's skeletal structure was out of alignment in several places. The golden supported my observation when I questioned her. She told me her trainer continued to ask her to do things that hurt, and she couldn't understand why. She finally bit her trainer in frustration. A trip to a local animal chiropractor later confirmed the misalignments in the dog's skeletal system.

STORMY

Katlyn called me regarding her thirteen year old Great Pyrenees dog, Stormy. Katlyn feared he was having a recurrence of an earlier bout of cancer, because he exhibited great pain.

I saw during a phone session that he had a rib out of place and recommended a chiropractic adjustment. After Katlyn located a pet chiropractor, she wrote the following to me:

> "On the way to the chiropractor, Stormy was in so much pain we had to pick him up and carry him to the car. Sure enough, there was a rib out of place. The chiropractor popped it back in, and Stormy got up and jumped back in the car by himself!"

Because alignment problems surface frequently in my readings, I have become an enthusiastic supporter of this type of treatment to relieve pain and improve health. In fact, my elderly dog, Trina, enjoyed regular chiropractic adjustments to enhance her comfort and well–being.

REMY

A combination of remedies relieved the symptoms of Lynda's wonderful little male Bichon, Remy. He had developed severe seizures for no apparent reason at the age of only a year and a half. Lynda called me in desperation to save her pet after she had already spent thousands of dollars on vets, tests, and animal specialists. She still had no diagnosis. I immediately saw that he was poisoned by additives in his popular expensive dog food.

I assured Remy that Lynda was going to be able to help him now. She switched his diet to a raw brand to start the healing and consulted with a holistic vet who flushed the toxins from Remy's body with acupuncture and herbs. The outcome—a happier and healthier dog.

CONCLUSION

Unwanted animal behaviors, such as aggression and destruction of property, are sometimes blamed on lack of training or the animal's defective breeding or background. Improper diet plays a major role in many of these cases. When the diet is replaced with fresh, nutritious, and unprocessed foods, the behavior often corrects automatically.

There appears to be an escalation of diet–related behavior problems among my clients' pets. Is this a sick symptom of a grab–and–go society? Do we value convenience over good health? It's much easier to serve processed food than to take time to prepare a meal with fresh ingredients. In fact, our own bodies reflect this same manifestation and for the same reason. We are moving too fast and not taking proper care of ourselves or our pets.

I discovered a new animal health resource for Trina when she was fourteen. Trina's nutritional needs changed as she aged. She required a different combination of herbs and food from what I had previously provided. My vet referred me to a holistic animal nutritional healer, Crista

Meyer. Crista eliminated Trina's symptoms with a change of food, supplements, and a particular type of exercise.

Investing in preventative health care provides a powerful tool for optimizing our animal companion's health. Suitable nutrition and exercise can add quality years to a pet's life, just as it does for humans. In addition, conventional animal health care professionals are increasingly utilizing holistic treatments such as acupuncture and energy therapies. The wide availability of herbal and homeopathic remedies, essential oils, and nutritional supplements also extend healing options. Sometimes, a little detective work is required to identify professionals skilled in these treatments; but, I assure you, they are plentiful and increasing in numbers. The resulting happy and healthy pet is well worth the extra effort required to seek out competent practitioners in your region.

CHAPTER FIVE

Behavior Changes:
What's in it For Me?

"Behavior is a mirror in which everyone displays his own image."

~ *Goethe*

A large portion of my work involves consultations with pet owners who want to change undesirable animal behavior. Aggressiveness, urinating and defecating in unacceptable areas, excessive barking or biting, and other neurotic behaviors send pet owners to the brink of madness. I become the "mediator" for these sessions. I must weed through a complex set of information to determine the root cause of the unwanted actions. I know from experience that humans complicate the situation with all their assumptions. The human tells me one story, the animal tells me another.

My first objective is to determine what type of behavior the human wants to change. I must strip away all the extraneous material relayed to me and separate out only the specific behavior that needs modification. To do this, I release judgment and place my consciousness in a state of neutrality. Then, I encourage the animal to express its likes and dislikes in a two–way conversation to establish rapport and foster trust. Once that is accomplished, I send the animal a picture of the specific behavior that is upsetting the human. As I listen to the animal's side of the story, I gather information about both the animal and the human in order to unearth negotiation tools for changing a behavior. Animals want to know, "What's in it for me?"

A miscommunication from the human usually fosters the unwanted behavior. We assume that animals think the same way we think. This is not true. Humans rely on spoken languages as their primary mode of communication. Animals rely on telepathy as their primary mode of communication. When the spoken words of humans do not match the thoughts and pictures in their heads, the incongruity confuses the animals and they tend to respond to the thoughts and pictures first.

Humans, as they speak, are not even aware they are generating information telepathically. I advise my human clients to improve their communication process by developing consistency with their thoughts and words. For example, if you suspect your dog is about to pee on the rug, don't say the words "go outside" while you are thinking (and picturing) he's about to pee on the rug. Instead, send the animal a mental picture of the preferred place for its bathroom duties with your verbal command.

The next step is to educate the humans concerning the animal's deep instincts. One way I approach this is to have the humans imagine putting their consciousness into the animal's body. They begin to understand how the animal experiences life from its point of view. While human agenda disconnects from nature, animals operate as an integral part of nature. Their rules for living are quite different. Many of our rules seem illogical and frustrating to them. Our ideas of clean living, such as no muddy paws on the freshly mopped floor, keeping pet food in the bowl, and not walking on the kitchen counters mystify them. They have their own criteria for behavior, most of which is based on their natural instincts.

Animals sense and respond to energies from living beings and other sources such as spaces, electronics, and weather. They are also bombarded with extraneous telepathic information from their humans. Humans don't realize they are creating superfluous messages, because they are so accustomed to their own habitual mental chatter. Communication with animals becomes easier as humans consistently replace their mental chatter with clear intention.

TO PEE OR NOT TO PEE

Jane called for help in preparing her two dogs— Samson, a King Charles Cavalier spaniel, and Macy, a yellow Labrador retriever—for an upcoming move to England. When I connected with the dogs they said: "Yeah, we know all about the move. We've seen the packed boxes, and we heard Mom on the phone making all the arrangements."

As an afterthought, Jane added that she wanted to modify a bathroom behavior. The dogs continually relieved themselves on the outside patio behind her home. This behavior could pose a greater problem in their new London home, for Jane had strict orders from her future landlord that her dogs must do all bathroom business on the periphery of the property.

I thought, *How am I going to get these dogs to go in the right place as this is not a natural dog behavior.* I asked Jane to describe what the new home looked like and exactly where she wanted the dogs to go. She suggested an area adjacent to the backyard fence. I relayed the information visually to the two dogs, but I received no strong response that they understood or would cooperate. I then added that the humans would be very impressed if they followed through with this change of behavior.

As we wrapped up the phone session, Jane suddenly exclaimed, "Oh my gosh!"

Her daughter had just let the dogs out in the backyard and they had immediately gone to relieve themselves in an area by the fence. I was very surprised at how quickly they grasped the concept, because I had spent most of the time showing them the London yard.

OLLIE BUBBA—B&B BULLY

Behavior problems can arise from multiple sources. Three factors created Ollie Bubba's aggressive attitude. When I entered a client's bed and breakfast inn for the first time, I heard the click click click of dog nails on tile coming toward me. A brown and white wire–haired Jack Russell terrier planted himself right in front of me with legs spread like an offensive lineman. He looked me in the eye and said point blank, "This is my house."

I am familiar with aggressive dogs, so I knew to hold my position and stay grounded. I shot back a famous Jim Carrey line, "Alrighty then."

My affirmative response caught him off-guard. "OK, as long as you know that." He backed up to let me pass.

I walked by him to meet Phaedra and Robert, his humans. Immediately, an angry female ghost approached me, who also said, "This is my house." Obviously, this ghost had been influencing the dog's bullying behavior. (I haven't discussed the subject of ghosts or spirits yet but will address this in a later chapter.)

At this point, I sat down with Phaedra and Robert to conduct the session. Ollie Bubba hopped up on the loveseat to indicate his leadership in the pack. Dogs will often seek out higher ground to display their alpha status. I connected with him and let him talk about his likes and dislikes, favorite foods, and most enjoyed activities. As he "talked," I discerned his gall bladder made him feel irritable. Poor diet caused this condition.

I asked Phaedra, "Are there any behavior problems you'd like to discuss?"

Immediately, Ollie Bubba stood up and growled at me. I stood up too, so I would appear taller, and I commanded him to get off the loveseat and onto the floor. He clearly confirmed his acceptance of my authority with his compliance.

Because Phaedra and Robert had not firmly established their roles as leaders, Ollie Bubba had stepped into the position to fulfill "dog rules." Once alerted to this expectation, Robert implemented the authority concept so effectively that Ollie Bubba transformed into a happy and relaxed companion right before our eyes.

Part one of addressing Ollie Bubba's aggression was encouraging the humans to assume the leadership role. Part two required a focus for his high energy. I asked him if he would adopt the role of host and greet everyone who came into the bed–and–breakfast. When Ollie Bubba immersed himself in these new duties, the lingering ghost's contributing energy became less influential. Part three of the cure addressed Ollie Bubba's nutritional needs. I recommended the raw diet, and encouraged Phaedra and Robert to use some of his favorite treats as a reward for desirable behavior.

This case illustrates how multiple components combine to create behavioral problems. Situations requiring several changes are common in my practice. Establishing clear leadership, giving the pet a specific job, and providing a proper diet emerge in combination as a recurring theme to improve many undesirable pet behaviors.

CAMERA–SHY DOG

Dahlia, a beautiful female Dalmatian, worked as a model for advertisements. Her problems emerged during photo shoots. As soon as the camera appeared, she would lower her head, back off, and try to hide. When I visited the home, I suggested her caretaker, Susan, bring out the camera so I could observe Dahlia's behavior. Dahlia looked for a place to hide as soon as the camera came into view.

I asked Dahlia, "Why are you reacting this way to the camera?"

She told me she previously resided with a guy in Alabama. The man had employed harsh and abusive methods to force her to be a hunting dog. The loud noise from the gun terrified her when he took her into the field for training.

Susan's large camera featured a telescopic lens, and Dahlia had transferred her fear from the gun to the camera.

At the first click of the camera, she immediately reacted as if a gun had fired. Her fear escalated to the point where the mere sight of the camera would trigger total anxiety.

I suggested that Susan leave the camera on the room's low coffee table all the time in order to desensitize Dahlia. I discovered that Dahlia liked Susan's perfume, so I proposed putting a little dab on the camera strap as an aid in the desensitization process. Dahlia loved Susan, and the scent would calm her.

Dahlia's story demonstrates that behavior modification with animals works somewhat differently than it works with humans. When Susan first showed the camera to Dahlia, and Dahlia reacted fearfully, Susan treated her like a child and tried to comfort her. Dahlia interpreted Susan's comfort as a reward for the behavior. Susan's attempts to placate Dahlia reinforced the anxiety behavior.

Dahlia was a rescued animal, and generally, humans tend to feel sorry for them. Remorse is a weakness in the animal world. An unbalanced animal requires a strong and confident leader. Clear and consistent training provides the animal with a feeling of security and an understanding of expected behavior. Strong, positive praise is the best response for desirable behavior. And again, I heartily stress that people work on maintaining congruency between their thoughts and words while speaking to animals.

LAST-CHANCE SHELTIE

A Texas nursing home called me regarding Max, a shelter dog they adopted to serve as a resident mascot. The elderly people in the nursing home loved Max. He returned their affection and felt responsible for their safety. However, Max had developed an aggressive attitude toward visitors. This created a serious predicament for the nursing home manager.

When I questioned Max, he expressed confusion about his job. He said there were some shady visitors coming to the nursing home and he was protecting his people. I told him it was not his job to protect the residents. If he detected shady people, he was to go to a safe place under the manager's desk and lie down. His job description was clarified so that he knew he was to provide companionship, not protection. I made sure he understood that any continuation of aggressive behavior would result in his euthanasia. Evidently, the negotiations with Max were successful, because the manager later told me Max had embraced his new role.

MARCO THE MAGNIFICENT

Phoebe called me to investigate the origin of the confrontational behavior of her male cat, Marco the Magnificent. Marco, a thirteen-pound Maine Coon, frequently snarled and hissed at the other cats in the household. Marco also viciously attacked Travis, an eleven-pound male chocolate Lynx/Siamese who had recently been brought indoors after recovering from an illness. The attacks resulted in knock–down drag–out fights that sometimes awakened Phoebe several times during the night. Phoebe loved Marco but was afraid she would have to give him up because of his persistent bullying.

She told me she believed in reincarnation and felt that we have things to learn in this life. She was sure that Marco had something to learn, and she wished to help him so that his next life would be better. I preferred to remain neutral.

Marco truly reflected his name. He exuded magnificence. A very smart and mischievous cat and proud of his body, Marco would strut around and posture in front of the other cats. He told me he "owned" Phoebe and that he was the "boss in the household." Marco said he was in Phoebe's life to reflect her emotional issues and assist her in recognizing her need to change. She did not like confrontation and would hold back her true feelings. He was taking on the energy of her accumulating frustration and acting it out for her. When I relayed this information to Phoebe, she acknowledged that she was reluctant to engage in any kind of conflict.

Then Travis entered the conversation. He described himself as very friendly, calm, harmonious, and respectful. He is comfortable alone, doesn't like confrontation, and can't set boundaries. When Phoebe affirmed this information, I realized that Travis mirrored Phoebe's passivity.

We decided to approach the issue on two levels, physical and energetic. Implementing a "time out" by removing Marco from the company of the other cats when he displayed aggression provided a temporary physical solution. In order to permanently change his behavior, Phoebe would have to tackle her own issues (i.e., her reluctance to express herself and set boundaries).

I know this sounds confusing, so here is a brief explanation of this principle. I have learned that the pairing of human and animal is no accident. Animals choose to come into relationships to help their humans learn something about themselves. Animals reflect energy generated by their humans. Humans must first change their own behaviors to effect change in animals' behaviors.

Beliefs, behaviors, thoughts, and feelings create a type of energy. This energy generates a field that can extend from the immediate environment out to the entire universe. Change anywhere in the energy field creates ripples that affect every being within the field. This explains how Phoebe's choice to express more power would directly influence Marco's behavior. As Phoebe's power increases, Marco's need to assert his authority decreases.

In a follow-up conversation, Phoebe told me Marco's behavior improves when she asserts herself and regresses when she resumes her old, passive behavior. I admire Phoebe's courage and willingness to work on self–change. Permanent change requires conscious decision and is a continuous process.

MIN PIN WITHOUT A SOUL

On occasion, I encounter soulless animals. You might wonder how an animal can exist without a soul. In my experience, an animal can function with minimal awareness and survive by instinct alone. The few soulless animals I have encountered have been extremely dangerous because they exist in a perpetual survival mode.

What is the purpose of these creatures in our world? Sometimes our best spiritual lessons come from difficult circumstances. The following story provides a perfect example.

A clinic arranged a day of readings for its clients. I walked into the waiting room where a Miniature Pinscher growled and snarled at me. I told him I was there to help his owner communicate with him, and this information calmed him. I excused myself from the room for a moment. When

I returned, he repeated his confrontational performance. I realized he did not remember me from just a few minutes earlier and that his behavior was purely instinctual. This dog had a very short memory and no soul. I sensed a total vacancy in his energy.

The woman brought in the Min Pin for a reading to identify the cause of his dangerous behavior. He viciously snapped at her children and friends, and had even snapped at her. I received intuitive information that the dog's menacing behavior represented a re–creation of an unresolved relationship issue from the woman's past.

She had endured this dog's negative behavior for eight years and admitted the dog posed a problem. She noticed the aggression when he was a small puppy and had adopted him because she felt no one else would take him. She felt sorry for him and couldn't let him go, even though his threatening behavior had substantially increased.

I recommended the dog be put down immediately, explaining that she did not need to feel remorse about this course of action. I told her the dog had no soul and no deep emotional attachments to anyone. He felt no love for her and he posed a serious physical threat to others. Keeping this dog would result in an attack and possibly a lawsuit.

Despite my warning, she declined to act on my advice. She allowed the dog to continue existing in his vacant state. Several months later I learned that the Min Pin bit someone and was euthanized.

CAT ARBITRATION

Dolores fostered thirteen cats and loved them all. She called me because one very large and recent addition,

Dexter, upset the social balance in her cat family by instigating terrible fights. She wanted to understand more about his background.

Dolores prepared the cats for my visit by telling them all that I would be coming to talk with them. To our surprise and delight, a row of cats lined up to greet me as I entered the property. They seemed eager for the chance to communicate with us.

The cats represented a cross section of personalities, from mild–mannered to very aggressive, as in Dexter's case. I interviewed all of them to get to the root of the problem. Dexter, as it turned out, was somewhat of a thug in the cat world. He lacked social cat graces and quite often targeted Michael, a mild–mannered ginger boy and quite a bit smaller in size. Dexter would have to modify his unacceptable behavior to remain in this cozy family.

I put on my psychic detective hat and discovered that Dexter was not entirely at fault. Michael turned out to be a smart aleck and would mouth off at Dexter, who would never back down from a fight. Michael called Dexter, "Ninny Boy." (Where do cats get these names?)

I appealed to Dex's better nature. I told him that even though he was not instigating the fight, he was the one who was causing the damage. He was "bigger than that." I said that he would have to go back to the shelter if he couldn't control himself. I also told Michael, "Please stop taunting Dexter so he won't have an excuse to hurt you."

Dolores was pleased with the outcome. Dexter modified his behavior. Although he continued to chase Michael or corner him, he would not "lay a paw" on Michael.

PREVENTIVE MEASURES

Creating a satisfying human/animal partnership requires a little planning. I have compiled a short list of suggestions that can prevent many undesirable behaviors. In addition, you may discover other preventive measures just by paying attention to the animal.

My suggestions:

1. Improve your pet's diet. A little research into appropriate natural foods, or a consultation with an excellent animal nutrition practitioner, can prevent many problems and keep your pet in optimal health.

2. Establish yourself as the leader.

3. Invest time in human/animal training. Pets and humans are happiest when they learn valuable communication techniques.

4. Continue to give praise once the animal learns the desired behavior.

5. Develop consistency between your thoughts and speech to eliminate conflicting messages. Purposely visualize the message you wish

to convey.

6. Look within yourself to ascertain qualities or energies that your pet may be reflecting back to you; i.e., behaviors, illnesses, emotions, etc.

The above points teach humans how to become mindful in interacting with their pets. This attention flows into every other area of life. For example, while researching your pet's food, you may decide to evaluate your own diet. As you improve your relationship with your pet, you may notice similarities with the way you interact with other humans. All the clues for developing a successful and spiritual life are right in front of us. Becoming mindful gives us 20/20 spiritual eyesight.

CHAPTER SIX

Lost and Rescued Pets

"I'm not lost."

~ Sunnie, a female Cairn terrier

LOST PETS

People have retained me to assist in finding missing pets. I no longer assist with finding these pets because frequently, when I made contact with the pets they said, "I'm not lost."

Pets stray for a variety of reasons. They may be bored with their environment so they look elsewhere for adventure. Or, they are fleeing from perceived danger so they seek a place of safety. Sometimes their egos get bruised and they run away to punish their humans. Some of the missing animals are stolen.

Domesticated animals possess dual identities. As soon as your pet steps out the door, it is greeted with an array of dizzying sights, sounds, and aromas as its primal nature takes over. Your precious pooch transforms into a primitive wolf and your cuddly lap kitty mutates into a stalking mountain lion. The oblivious human expects a pet to follow an established routine. What a shock to discover the trustworthy pet has responded to a call of the wild! Chasing wildlife, investigating unfamiliar scents and seeking out companionship are natural reactions to stimuli. These behavioral mechanisms have been encoded into their DNA. Instincts can overwhelm the best-trained animals and influence them to wander.

Two levels of experience occur simultaneously with animals. One is physical, the other is spiritual. On the physical level, pets stray, find another place to live, or return to their original home.

They are following a different and greater plan on the spiritual level. In addition to developing their own souls, animals enter and leave our lives to help us learn our soul lessons. They may move on because they have accomplished their mission. Or, they have reached an impasse with the humans' progress. Their frustration rises when humans cling stubbornly to negative habits. At that point, some animals feel compelled to leave to further their own soul evolution.

Pets often have multiple assignments. For example, I was the fourth home for my dog Trina. Through an amazing string of synchronistic events covering a distance of 400 miles and including three cities, she arrived in my life exactly when I needed her assistance in making major life changes and growing spiritually.

RUN FOR YOUR LIFE

Brenda, a vet tech, called me to locate her cat. Earlier, she had been in a rush to get to work and had snatched up her husband's cat to take it into the house. In response, the cat bit her so hard she dropped him and he ran away. When I made contact with the cat, he told me he was fine. I could see a white wooden house owned by an elderly woman who left bowls of food and water on her porch for stray cats. A crisscross patterned fence surrounded the yard, and I sensed the property was near Brenda's home. I asked the cat to stay visible so his humans could find and retrieve him.

He replied, "I don't want to go home."

"Why not?"

"Because Brenda is going to kill me."

Brenda burst out crying when I gave her this information. She told me, when the cat bit her, she angrily blurted out, "I'm going to euthanize you." She was sorry she made the comment and had no intention of following through with her threat.

She and her husband eventually located the house with the crisscross fence. When they showed a photo of the cat to the elderly woman who lived there, she said she recognized him and had been feeding him. Although they repeatedly searched the neighborhood, the cat was never seen again. Apparently, he meant what he said.

The incident resulted in a positive outcome in spite of the loss of the cat. Brenda gained a deeper understanding of the keen awareness of animals. She now had the opportunity to become much more mindful of her own responsibility in cultivating trust in her future relationships with animals.

WINNIE THE POOH

The following account is from my client Ava:

"My cat, Winnie the Pooh, liked to hang out on the patio of my apartment. When he was 13 years old, he suddenly decided to leave the safety of the enclosed patio and roam around the apartment complex. I was beside myself because he had been gone for two days and I was leaving the next day to go out of town. In desperation, I called Myra. I could barely speak when she answered the phone.

"Myra, Pooh is missing."

"Ava, missing animals are very hard to find. They tell me where they are according to what they literally see in their immediate environment."

I wanted Myra to try anyway. She connected with him and he showed her a swimming pool. She asked me if there was a pool nearby.

"Yes, there are several in the complex."

Pooh told Myra that he was hanging out by the pool with some guys that were very nice.

Myra relayed my request that he come home immediately.

Pooh said, "Tell her I'll be home in a minute."

Myra told me his statement was odd because animals' concept of time is different from ours.

I had a going–away party to attend that evening so I left my back door open, just in case Pooh came home. I returned home around 2:00 AM and decided to go outside to call him one more time. Lo and behold, the little brat was right outside in the bushes! I picked him up and just cried and cried. When we got inside, I told him that he was grounded for two weeks. I swear he rolled his eyes at me. I stuck to my guns and, when the two weeks were up, he was meowing at the door. I turned to him and said, "In a minute, in a minute!" I laughed as I realized that I was the source of his comment to Myra!

ALABAMA DACHSHUNDS

A woman from Alabama called me to locate two dachshunds that were missing from her fenced and secured backyard. I determined that a criminal couple had stolen the friendly dogs. They worked as professional dognappers to collect financial rewards, either for the sale of dogs or the dogs' return. I cautioned my client to be very careful in retrieving her dogs as the dangerous couple could be easily provoked. I advised her to advertise a reward through a local media contact with which I intuitively felt she knew. She should quickly pick up the dogs with no questions asked when the couple called her.

The woman followed my instructions and soon received the call from the couple. As she drove up to the address, she recognized the house from my description. Her two dogs came running to her from under the house porch as soon as she stepped from her car. They had gotten outside earlier and refused to come out from under the porch when the couple tried to retrieve them. She immediately paid the couple and promptly left with both dogs safe and sound.

STRAYS

Some people think that a stray enters one's life as a random event. My experience indicates there is always a purpose behind the union between human and animal.

SALEEM THE JESTER

My client Lea walked her little male Westie, Griffin, every day for their mutual exercise. On one of her walks, a large but noticeably thin mixed–breed dog followed her home despite her best attempts to ignore him. The dog stayed in her yard for hours, so she eventually offered him food and water. When the dog greeted her in the morning, she and her husband decided they would care for him until they could return him to his home. Despite their efforts to find his home by posting flyers with his photo all around the area, no one claimed the beautiful animal. Since he displayed such a friendly and gentle nature, they decided to welcome him as a permanent family member.

When I talked to Saleem, he told me he had joined the family to bring in a sense of fun and lightness and to provide an example of being in the flow of the "now" moment. Lea and her husband had been facing some life challenges, and Griffin reflected his caretakers' tense energy. Saleem's easygoing personality reminded them not to worry so much. His antics kept everyone on their toes and amused. Saleem's job as a jester helped balance the energies in the household.

DIANA'S DILEMMA

Diana's kind heart led her to rescue so many dogs that her finances were stretched to the limit. Finally, a large English sheepdog entered her life and needed $10,000 worth of medical care. Diana expressed extreme distress over the decision on whether to proceed with the costly procedures.

I offered a different point of view.

"I've learned from the animals that there is always a spiritual lesson, and the lesson for you is that it is enough to do what you can within your means to make the dog comfortable for the remainder of his life. Approach this in a positive way by cultivating an attitude of acceptance and knowing that you can't fix everything."

This experience sparked Diana's interest in her own spiritual development. At this point, she created a new and better life for herself. The dog eventually healed with minimal intervention. I have no doubt that Diana's happiness contributed to the change in the dog's health.

THE KITTY CONNECTION

Dolores (mentioned earlier in the story about cat arbitration) acquired another cat in an unusual manner. She found a kitten sitting in the center of a turn lane on a major highway. He looked as if he was waiting for her. Of course she picked him up.

Tommy, the small brown rescued tabby, was 1½ years old when I visited Dolores' household to read her cat family. Dolores' longtime friend Angela was present during the communication session. I then discovered Tommy's life mission.

Tommy told me he was "assigned" to Angela, that he was "her" cat even though he lived with Dolores. The information did not surprise Angela and Dolores. Dolores described the change in Tommy's behavior every time Angela comes to visit from her home in Norway. During her long visits, which last from six weeks to three months, he remains Velcroed to Angela's side. He only fraternizes with the other cats when she leaves.

I asked Angela, "Would you consider giving Tommy a permanent home?"

"Yes, but I regularly make very long trips between Norway and the US. He would have to stay in Norway."

"I'll ask Tommy if he is OK with that."

Tommy perked up. "I hear there are a lot of fish in Norway!" His cute response reflected knowledge he received from Angela.

Tommy also connected me with Angela's deceased husband, Erik. Before he died from colon cancer, Angela had agreed to move to his home country. He had been terribly homesick. Now he wanted to express his thanks for her gracious consent to relocate from her home in the United States to Norway.

Angela reacted emotionally to this information because she had been troubled about her husband's welfare after he passed. She gained tremendous comfort in receiving verifiable information about him, and knowing that he was in a wonderful and peaceful place without pain.

Later, I learned that neither Angela nor Erik had any interest in cats before they met Tommy. They had become acquainted with him when he was still a kitten during their long visits with Dolores. Tommy taught both of them the joy of cat companionship. After Erik passed, Tommy's affection for Angela grew stronger.

She now returns his affection by letting him sleep on her bed and giving him special treats and toys. He gently touches her face with his paw at night and rolls over to let her stroke his belly, a privilege he does not extend to anyone else.

Angela decided that it was impractical to travel internationally with Tommy, so he continues to live as a special guest at Dolores' home. He enjoys a dual life, one as Angela's pampered companion when she visits, and the other as a member of Dolores's cat gang when Angela is absent.

It appears this little stray kitten that "accidentally" wandered into Dolores' life through a string of synchronicities, played a powerful part in establishing a communication between a loving wife and her deceased husband.

CHAPTER SEVEN

Deceased Pets

"Whatsoever that be within us that feels, thinks, desires and animates is something celestial and divine and consequently imperishable."

~ Aristotle

When animals leave their physical bodies, they pass over to the spiritual dimension, just like humans. Pets and humans in soul form often stay in contact with living loved ones.

REBA AND RJ

Reba grew increasingly despondent because her longtime companion, a male poodle named RJ, was assisted in exiting his body after battling diabetes for many years. She felt tremendous guilt over the euthanasia. The clinic that treated RJ referred Reba to me as they were concerned about her continued and increasing melancholy.

I contacted RJ, and he expressed concern regarding Reba's health. RJ mentioned that he loved her and continued to act as her protector. RJ added that he was really glad to be out of that body and that Reba had made the correct decision to end his physical suffering. He also gave me personal information that deeply affected her.

The reading comforted Reba regarding RJ's welfare in the afterlife. Reba decided to continue readings on a monthly basis because she had been so closely connected to RJ. Each time, RJ would give her information about current events she was experiencing—something as simple as mentioning that she had the broken dishwasher repaired. In that way, RJ was showing her that he stayed close to her in spirit. Reba derived great solace from the sessions, and gradually her anxiety lessened. Her outlook brightened when she took RJ's advice and began to travel. Eventually she moved on with her life and did not need continual reassurance from monthly readings.

RJ's story depicts a recurring theme of guilt in my readings when people decide to euthanize an animal. I have never had an animal express sadness or anger about being released from its body by its loved one. The animal remains with us in a spirit form and still loves us and watches over us. While we are the ones who struggle with the idea of death and the afterlife, animals are already fully aware of the process of birth and death as equal partners in the flow of life. They accept physical death as a natural transition to another form of existence.

People often misinterpret a pet's reactions during euthanasia. Humans project their own fear of death onto the animal. When they see the beloved pet looking frightened, they think the animal is afraid to die. Usually the animal's visible distress is a reflection of the human's fearful energy.

Humans can ease the transition by creating a more positive experience during euthanasia. Express love and appreciation and assure your pet you will be OK. The kindest and most loving parting gift that honors an animal is permitting him/her to move on.

BETSY AND GLORY

The day came to help Betsy's favorite elderly golden retriever transition to the afterlife. I accompanied the vet to help prepare for the event. Glory held a special place in the family. She was the matriarch of their dog pack, just as Betsy was her counterpart for the human family. She and Betsy maintained a very close bond and, when Betsy confronted a serious illness, Glory also deteriorated. The time had come to assist Glory in her transition to the afterlife.

A decision was made to administer the drugs on the big bed where the dogs and their humans slept in one big pack every night. I relayed information from the vet to Glory about the process so she would know what to expect. Animals seem to appreciate this information. Glory's last request, when she saw us preparing the bed by laying towels over the covers, was the desire to relieve herself outside. She did not want to risk soiling the beautiful comforter on Betsy's bed. Glory still acted as the caring matriarch for her extended family even while preparing for her own departure. I was deeply moved by her unwavering concern and devotion to her family.

BUCKWHEAT

Sometimes our animals deliberately delay their passing to accommodate our feelings and needs. A client contacted me by telephone and asked me to communicate with Buckwheat, a 30–year–old mare that resided on her West Texas ranch.

Buckwheat gave me the following information. Some horses she had been close to were gone, and she missed them. She was tired. It was hard for her to stand at times, and her heart was weak. There was a man around her who acted tough although he was soft inside. He remained very attached to her. He talked to her all the time, and she felt sad about leaving him. She hung on to life just for him. She adored him and was grateful for all his attention. She needed to know that he would be OK when she passed over.

My client identified the man—the ranch foreman. I suggested the foreman share his emotions with Buckwheat and release her so she could go in peace. The foreman complied with the advice and talked to Buckwheat later in the day. When he walked out to the pasture the next morning, he discovered that Buckwheat had passed on.

JAVA'S LAST ADVENTURE

Karen called me when she could not locate her aging cat. Java usually stayed upstairs because she was afraid of the downstairs cat, Bitty Bit. Earlier that day, Java had boldly ventured downstairs to eat Bitty Bit's food—very strange behavior as Bitty Bit terrorized Java every time Java entered her domain. Karen scolded Java for eating Bitty Bit's food and Java fled back upstairs. Karen followed her with concern that something was amiss. She checked Java for any possible injury, and the cat seemed OK. Later that day, Java vanished.

When I made contact with Java, she had already died. She said she had known she was dying and decided to have one last fling. She planned to do the things she always wanted to do. She ate some of the food she knew she was not supposed to eat. Later in the day, she noticed the door ajar and darted out to freedom to a nature preserve behind the house. Eventually, she grew tired, then just lounged in the tall green grass. She happily breathed her last breath as she watched the nearby birds and insects. Java assured me she had not died a violent death due to any attack by dogs or coyotes.

Java had taken a positive view of her last day on earth. Instead of focusing on her impending transition, she lived her remaining time to the fullest by throwing caution to the wind for one last exhilarating adventure.

LIVING LIFE ON THE EDGE

Baxter was a cat who chose a risky lifestyle versus a life of boredom. His human guardian called me to make contact with him after he died. She felt distressed and somehow partly responsible for his death. I contacted him, and he told me he was in a great place, a cat heaven.

"How did you die?" I asked.

He showed me that he liked to walk along the top of the fence that adjoined the neighbor's yard. He enjoyed teasing the two pit bulls next door. On his last day of life, he worked them into such a frenzy the dogs succeeded in pulling him down from the fence.

Lena confirmed the circumstances of Baxter's death and said she felt guilty because she had allowed him to roam free. She thought he might have lived longer than 3 ½ years had she kept him indoors at all times.

At this point, Baxter expressed gratitude that she had allowed him independence. He had lived a short, but very happy lifetime. Then he showed me something else.

I asked Lena, "Did you have another male cat that was hit by a car and died?"

"Yes, Jaxson."

I told her that Baxter showed me that Jaxson greeted him as he crossed over.

Baxter's comments soothed Lena. The cats reversed her previous viewpoint, that longevity is more important than quality of life. Lena released her guilt surrounding Baxter's death. Knowing that Jaxson had assisted Baxter in his transition provided her with additional comfort.

REGARDING GRIEF

Clients often call me to speak with pets that have crossed over. I am especially happy to provide this service because, in most cases, it teaches people that life does not end when the body ceases to function. When they receive information from their deceased pets, they realize their beloved pets are still around—however, in a different form. Most people then understand that their pets abide in a happy and loving environment, a little piece of animal heaven. Subsequently, people are able to move on after the initial grieving and cherish the memories of their beloved pets.

Occasionally, I encounter clients who have difficulty moving through a loss. They rehash every detail of the event and beat themselves up for what they did or did not do. Those stuck in grief should consider counseling. It's easier to move forward emotionally once we acknowledge our fears and deal with them.

It's also important to note that one individual's suffering affects everyone. Our thoughts, feelings, and beliefs create our personal energy field, whether negative or positive, and affect the collective energy of the universe. So addressing our fears concerning death is a wonderful and courageous accomplishment and contributes to the betterment of the energy of the world. This accomplishment also honors the positive impact of the pets in our lives.

CHAPTER EIGHT

Do You See What I See?

"For death is no more than a turning of us over from time to eternity."

~ *William Penn*

In my experience, animals always sense presences we can't see. Sometimes, what we interpret as mysterious behavior in animals can be their reaction to those invisible energies. The most unexpected aspects of my work with animals have been encounters with spirits, ghosts, and the mysterious.

SPOOKY ENCOUNTERS

MANDY AND THE HAUNTED HOUSE

Mandy, the black Lab, didn't want to go home when I talked to her at a local veterinary clinic. She exhibited extreme anxiety at her impending release. The staff assumed she was upset because she thought her humans had abandoned her at the clinic. In fact, Mandy was well aware that her humans were coming to take her home, and that's what terrified her. She linked me directly with her house. I observed a multitude of menacing dark entities residing in the structure. The entities were affecting the owner's health and prosperity. When I mentioned this, the clinic manager commented on my insight. Mandy's human mother had complained to her about the new house being haunted, and she recently had been diagnosed with breast cancer.

I recommended to the clinic manger that the couple's best course of action was to sell the house and move at once. At first, Mandy's humans stayed since they had invested most of their savings in this beautiful dream home. But, they moved after a harrowing experience with a terrifying presence in the kitchen in the middle of the night.

Incidentally, the homes on both sides of the haunted house were put up for sale at approximately the same time because of similar problems.

RAT HAUNTING

Sometimes the ghosts are animals. My veterinarian friend once worked long shifts at an animal emergency clinic. An upstairs room in the clinic contained a bed so the staff could sleep and relax between cases. The entire staff agreed that the room was unpleasant, although for no discernible reason.

I evaluated the room's energy when I visited the clinic. An increasingly uncomfortable presence met me on a dark narrow stairway leading to the room's door.

When I entered the room, I asked, "Who are you?"

The energy identified itself as a little white male rat, and he was furious! He told me he had died at this clinic as a result of subterfuge. The rat had been brought into the emergency clinic by his loving male caretaker for a serious and sudden illness. As the rat's story unfolded, I learned that the man's new girlfriend did not like rats. When the man insisted on keeping his favorite pet, she had poisoned it. The little rat had died before the staff could diagnose the cause of his condition. He continued his existence as a ghost because he held onto his rage. Sometimes spirits, both human and animal, can become earthbound after they experience trauma.

I told the little rat that his purpose with the man had been fulfilled. I reminded him that the woman had created her own karma and she would not get away with her crime. Perhaps the man would figure it out at some point in the future, since the clinic had suspected the involvement of some type of poison. I encouraged the rat to move on, and he decided to leave peacefully.

The atmosphere of the room immediately improved with the departure of the rat. As an additional measure, we applied some *feng shui* principles by moving some of the furniture to change the feel of the room. *Feng shui* is the art of arranging objects to enhance the flow of energy and bring balance to a space. Afterward, the staff found the room so rejuvenating they competed over whose turn it was to grab a nap on the bed.

THE COWBOY GHOST

I talked with two mares on a ranch in southwest Texas. They reported that a manly ghost visited them all the time because he loved horses and still wanted to care for them. They described him as a Hispanic man who wore a cowboy hat and carried a lasso.

Unfortunately for him, his ghostly form spooked the horses. They shied away from him when he visited because they knew he didn't belong there. They would spot him over their shoulders and then sidle away from him with wide eyes.

When I relayed this information to the the ranch owners, they laughed. It explained some curious behavior they had observed in the horses. They were familiar with stories about the cowboy ghost circulated by neighboring ranchers. This example is typical of animals' sensitivities to the presence of spirits.

LEO'S INTERVENTION

Leo, a Maine Coon cat, lived with Mary and Alex in the Houston area. He adored his lady cat friend, Miss Isabelle. She resided in New Orleans but would often come to visit Mary and Alex with her caretaker, Paulette. Shortly before one of their scheduled visits, Leo's behavior changed radically. He exhibited irritability and relieved himself outside the litter box. That prompted Mary and Alex to set up an appointment with me to determine the root cause of Leo's problem.

Leo told me, "Paulette and Miss Isabelle would be better off staying with us permanently. I am connected with Miss Isabelle all the time and I can't protect her when she is in New Orleans."

"Why do you feel she needs protection?"

"Paulette's energy is being siphoned off by some kind of bad entity that lives in her house. It causes her to feel tired and overwhelmed. Miss Isabelle is taking on some of that bad energy in an effort to protect Paulette."

As I spoke with Leo, the entire picture presented itself to me. I knew that the negative energy affected both Paulette's and Miss Isabelle's health. They would need to clear out this spirit for everyone's well–being. I recommended a reputable and successful dowser to accomplish this task.

Clearly, Leo had developed a strategy to deal with an unpleasant situation that impacted everyone. He knew that Mary and Alex would call me if he misbehaved, and he would be able to enlighten them as to the danger to Miss Isabelle.

An unexpected bonus occurred as a result of the dowser's clearing. Paulette reported that, after repeated failed attempts to cultivate a healthy garden, her plants miraculously bloomed.

VISITATIONS

Our deceased pets show us their presence in a variety of ways. We can experience their spirit through touch, sound, smell, emotion, or visual manifestation. They communicate from the other side to let us know they are still with us. They may visit to protect us, teach other animals in our household, comfort us during emotional turmoil, or just hang out to see what is happening in our lives. I mention this because they reveal themselves so often in my consultations.

TWO SCOTTIES

A couple brought their Scotty to me for a reading at an animal charity fundraising event. The dog told me he didn't understand why his female caretaker remained so sad regarding the recent death of her other Scotty. He said the deceased dog visited her often in spirit form. The spirit Scotty would come around whenever she lit her candle.

Surprised at this information, his caretaker told me she had brought her remaining dog to me because she thought he might be depressed at the loss of his friend. She also revealed that lighting her aromatherapy candle helped her to feel better when she was sad. The news that her deceased dog was still around lifted her spirit. This communication underscores how animals understand and accept the transition process more easily than humans.

SADIE AND LIBBY

Sadie, an energetic Silky Terrier, runs over to Ellen's sliding glass door every evening at dusk and barks furiously at apparently nothing. I told Ellen that Sadie barks at another "ghost dog" that comes around to watch and check in on the family. Upon hearing this, Ellen remembered that her wonderful Australian shepherd, Libby, would make rounds and look in the very same window every evening at dusk before she passed away at the age of eighteen. Her appearance at the window would send Sadie into fits of confrontational barking. Ellen now recognized Sadie's distinctive bark at "the nothing" as the same bark she used toward Libby.

Thanks to Sadie, the dog medium, Ellen feels comfort knowing that Libby is still on guard.

CASPER

At a recent house call, I talked with three pugs about their health issues. During our exchange, I felt a distinct bump on my left thigh, like a dog bumping me with his nose. I was sitting on a dining room chair, and there was nothing else visible in the area. The pugs were too short to reach that spot. A large white dog sent me his image. I asked the client if a large white male dog that had a habit of poking people with his nose had previously lived with the family.

She said, "Yes, that was Casper, our Great Pyrenees. We called him the bottle–nosed dolphin because he bumped everyone with his nose, especially when he wanted attention."

MARBI AND THE MYSTERY MUSIC

In another case, I visited Angela's dog, Marbi, to determine if the very ill and deteriorating dog was ready to pass over. Marbi told me she wasn't quite ready but her time was near. Marbi said she would always be around or near Angela in spirit.

When Angela asked me how she would know when Marbi visited, Marbi said, "Tell her she'll hear music from no apparent source."

Angela immediately exclaimed, "That happened shortly before you arrived!"

Marbi confirmed that the music Angela heard was a test run to establish a specific signal for her future visitations. This manifestation is unusual for an animal still living, but I believe Marbi received assistance from her angels.

PERSIAN TALE

My clients, Richard and Alexia, surround themselves with a collection of dogs and cats. On one visit, they showed me a photograph of Richard's favorite cat, Ashley, now deceased. When I connected with the large Persian mix, she gave me specific information so Richard would know we were truly communicating. She told me she hangs around Richard all the time, even when he travels and stays overnight in hotels. Ashley said she lies on the bed and tickles him with her tail.

Richard laughed. "So that's where the tickling comes from. I feel it on my nose every night!"

A MEMORABLE GIFT

During a phone session, a deceased black Lab told me she would run to the kitchen every time someone opened the refrigerator door. Although she offered other specific details, the information did not satisfy the client's expectations.

She commented, "That information could pertain to any dog."

Since she couldn't accept that I was talking to her Lab, I asked the dog for something significant that the woman would recognize.

The dog said, "I'm around her all the time. Tell her she'll know when I'm close because she'll smell my gas."

When I reluctantly relayed this to the woman she burst out, "Now I know you're for real because that dog had the most obnoxious gas during her entire life."

That poor woman would now have to smell her dog's gas whenever the dog's spirit visited!

FAMILY REUNION

Pets frequently set up opportunities to facilitate communication between living and deceased loved ones. Therefore, I am often greeted by unexpected visitors during my appointments.

For instance, on one house call, I visited a family— a husband, wife, and their young children—to talk with their newly adopted kittens. As soon as I walked into the house, the husband's deceased father greeted me at the door. He wanted his son to know that he had not missed any important events in their lives and he was very proud of all of them. The true purpose of the session evolved into a reunion between father and son. The family was very happy to hear from grandpa, and his son felt more peace regarding the loss of his father.

MEETING THE MYSTERIOUS

I don't purposely seek out information about the strange and unusual. I know there is a lot of weird stuff out there but I prefer not to draw those energies to me unnecessarily. The universe will arrange important encounters that advance my spiritual education.

WOODY'S JITTERS

Samantha and Bill live on a remote farm of twenty acres bordering a national forest. Their philosophy is to live in harmony with nature and they hold a boundless love for animals both domestic and wild. As their friend, I have long been familiar with their domestic brood of four large dogs and nine cats.

Samantha requested that I come to talk with Woody, a smart, athletic, Rottweiler mix with a strong personality. Woody enjoys family evenings when the dogs gather comfortably in the living room with Samantha and Bill. Typically, the dogs snooze in their beds as the humans watch wildlife on deer cameras.

Woody suddenly exhibited periodic reversals of his normal confidence. He would cower and slink down to the end of the hallway to hide. Samantha said she wanted to know the source of his discomfort because none of the other dogs reacted to whatever was bothering Woody.

I sat down with Woody and said, "Woody, what's up?"

Very clearly he said, "I don't like it!"

"What are you talking about? You don't like what?"

"That thing."

"Send me what you're feeling so I can see what it feels like."

At that moment, I received a really jagged energy that seemed in constant motion, and it confused me.

"Oh, I don't like it either."

In the same instant I figured out what it was— Woody sent me a picture of a Bigfoot.

I turned to Samantha. "You're going to think I'm crazy, but he is showing me Bigfoot. He knows Bigfoot is really close every time he feels that energy."

Samantha, a very sensitive and intuitive person, said she always felt they were on the property although she was not threatened by them. She added, "We acknowledge their existence and will not disturb them."

When I talked to the other dogs, they confirmed that they sometimes sensed the same creature in the area. However, it did not bother them.

I recommended that Samantha and Bill just let Woody take care of himself. She agreed.

Two weeks later, the couple stopped to participate in a roadside survey near their home conducted by an official from the National Forest Service. After completing the survey they learned he was an employee of a nearby university, and they chatted about area hiking trails. The official asked them if they had seen a "Bigfoot," as there had been several reports of sightings in the area very close to their farm. They did not tell him what Woody had told me.

Weeks later, I talked with Simon, a newly acquired stray dog Samantha found in the woods. One of the first things Simon showed me was a picture of a Bigfoot.

He asked, "What the hell is that?"

Everyone laughed. I assured him that it will not bother him if he leaves it alone.

The above stories are typical of the diversity I encounter in readings. A type of energy, known or unknown, will reveal itself if one remains centered in a neutral and fearless state of nonjudgment. I continue to encounter all kinds of astonishing energies from other dimensions.

CHAPTER NINE

The Funny Side of Animals

"Humor is a serious thing. I like to think of it as one of our greatest earliest natural resources, which must be preserved at all cost."

~ *James Thurber*

PETS SAY THE DARNDEST THINGS

It pays to retain a sense of humor in this job because I never know what the animals will tell me. For instance, one day I was jogging through the park when I passed a mounted policeman. I sent the impressive sorrel horse under him a quick mental compliment: *My, you are a handsome horse.*

He shot back, "Can you tell him he's gained twenty pounds, and he's breaking my back?"

I acknowledged his request (proper etiquette in the animal world) and explained why I had to decline to pass on the information. Needless to say, I just continued my run a little faster.

Our furred and feathered friends are not always compassionate to other species, particularly their predators. While visiting a veterinary emergency clinic that housed several exotic finches in the surgery room, I asked the birds how they liked living at the clinic.

They responded, "We love it, especially when the cats come in for surgery."

At that moment, a cat under anesthesia lay spread eagle and motionless on a surgery table. Quite a mirthful image for those birds!

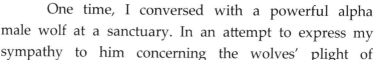

One time, I conversed with a powerful alpha male wolf at a sanctuary. In an attempt to express my sympathy to him concerning the wolves' plight of declining numbers, I said, "There are too many humans diminishing your habitat. "

Kahn looked me right in the eye and quickly responded, "Let me out of here, and I can fix that."

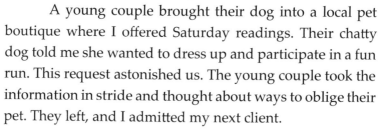

A young couple brought their dog into a local pet boutique where I offered Saturday readings. Their chatty dog told me she wanted to dress up and participate in a fun run. This request astonished us. The young couple took the information in stride and thought about ways to oblige their pet. They left, and I admitted my next client.

I emerged from the room much later. The couple stood waiting for me. They wanted to tell me that a woman entered the store just after their reading to distribute fliers advertising a fun run for dogs. It benefitted the local Humane Society and encouraged participants to dress their dogs in costumes. Did this canny dog set us up, or was it the law of synchronicity at work? I think it was both.

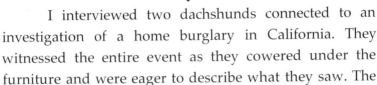

I interviewed two dachshunds connected to an investigation of a home burglary in California. They witnessed the entire event as they cowered under the furniture and were eager to describe what they saw. The problem was that they only portrayed the burglars from the knees down. They gave an explicit account of the criminals' jeans, color of their socks, and the type of shoes worn. The dogs also described the bottom of the get-away vehicle, a gray van.

Animals tend to be straight–to–the–point and not always especially genteel. Jasper, a meticulously groomed and dressed mare, performs in Western pleasure competitions. She is the horse equivalent of a diva. When I talked with her at the show, she communicated with a string of cuss words. As the horses lined up for the competition, she added, "Damn it. Get that horse's stinky butt out of my face."

The first thing Camo, a tiny and cute male Chihuahua, bragged to me in his Texas accent was, "I'm a huntin' dog!" He showed me a deer blind, but I thought he might be exaggerating.

When I asked his humans if they took him hunting, they casually responded, "Oh, yes. He sits on a shelf in the deer blind and he quietly lets us know when the deer are within range."

A Bichon Frise with a foot phobia puzzled his owners. They would set him on their laps when they entered their pool, and as long as they sat upright on their inflatable rafts, he was happy. As soon as they lay on their backs, the dog barked frantically and attacked their feet.

The dog told me he was trying to keep his owners from dying. Dead animals lie on their backs with feet pointed up. He thought his humans might drown.

It turns out that some animals have a sense of humor. A mischievous horse liked to play a favorite trick on his human. He would pretend he was dead by lying on his back with feet straight up whenever she arrived at the pasture. I told him to knock it off, as his prankster antics were wearing thin and greatly upsetting the kind lady.

Three schnauzers I visited kept insisting, "We're famous!"

They boasted about their framed photo that hung in a public place.

Their baffled humans could not think of any association between the dogs and the public.

When the dogs showed me the word "Hollywood" the humans made the connection. The store they owned included the word "Hollywood" in its name. They had prominently displayed a photo of the dogs on the store wall among a collection of famous movie art posters.

My client Kari decided to adopt a female companion for her Lab, Sampson. She thought it would be cute to call the new lady friend Delilah.

When I told Sampson what Kari was planning, he said, "No way! I want a boy dog so we can be best buddies and play really rough."

I suggested that Kari take Sampson with her to pick out his companion. Sampson selected Sinbad, a black male Lab, as his new best buddy. Kari told me they loved to roughhouse like typical boys.

Valentino is a gorgeous elegant black–and–white Great Dane with an interesting vocation. He serves as the mascot for an automobile dealership in its advertising and assists the executive staff with their duties. He also exudes a sophisticated sense of fashion. When I spoke with him, he indicated his desire to wear a black–and–white tux for an upcoming photo shoot. The dealership owner, Jill, remembered that she had bought one for him several years ago. Delighted, she agreed that Tino in a Tux provided a perfect image for the business.

Sam, the snitch, ratted out his male caretaker. This cute Cavalier King Charles Spaniel told me to tell his female caretaker, a holistic nutritionist with a Ph.D., that her husband's favorite food was Fritos and he sneaked them when she wasn't around. When she later confronted her surprised hubby, he confessed.

POWERFUL PRINCESS

A family called me to discover the source of an aggression problem with their female Lab. Chelsea and her sibling Beau were meant to be hunting dogs. Beau demonstrated strong hunting instincts. Chelsea did not, so she eventually was excluded from hunting trips.

Chelsea's female caretaker began to treat her more like a family dog. When she attempted to include Chelsea on walks around the neighborhood, Chelsea exhibited signs of alarming aggression to her and the children.

When I talked to Chelsea, she made it clear that she was a working dog and she didn't want to be a pet. She wanted to be taken seriously. Chelsea didn't like her frou frou name—she wanted to be called Ralph.

Her male caretaker chuckled when I shared this. He accepted keeping her as a hunting dog, although he didn't think the name Ralph was suitable for a female. I suggested that the name Xena might be more appropriate. Chelsea agreed to be called Xena, in lieu of Ralph, after I explained that Xena was a warrior princess. No one had an inkling of where she picked up the name, Ralph, until the family noticed a "Ralph" at a kennel where they often boarded her. I later learned that our negotiations were successful and Xena appeared much happier.

SPECIAL REQUESTS

I visited a scientist, Nora, who cared for German shorthaired pointers, along with some rescued strays. One of her winning show dogs, Daredevil, sent me very clear pictures of his special food request, a Payday candy bar. I didn't think I heard him correctly!

However, Nora admitted that she gave him little pieces of her favorite candy bar as rewards when he was young during obedience training. He hadn't forgotten about those sweet rewards. We negotiated the preferred behavior changes, to which he agreed, only if we restored Payday as his reward.

Daredevil's housemate Kenyon showed me that Cheez Whiz was her favorite treat.

Nora expressed amusement at this for she would give Kenyon a little of this soft cheese on crackers as a treat. Furthermore, she told me about the day she had left a can out on the kitchen counter and when she came home there was Cheez Whiz all over the room, including the ceiling. Kenyon had somehow managed to grab the can and puncture it. Apparently, cheese under pressure in aerosol cans can shoot about twenty feet!

A third request in this household came from Twister, who liked whipped cream out of the can. It seems that dogs are just as particular as humans when it comes to favorite foods.

One more request came from Nora's adopted stray. Riddle, a male, wore a plain collar, but he wanted to wear hot pink! This contrasted with a reading I did with another client's bulldog. Gracie, a female, removed and buried her pink collars. She adamantly expressed her desire to wear blue because she was not a "girly" dog. We can amend the famous O. Henry quote from "Clothes make the man" to "Collars make the dog."

MAVERICK

One time I stood at a ranch fence observing some alpacas. Moose, one of the ranch dogs, approached me with the desire to talk.

"How are you doing?" I asked.

"I'm a working dog."

"Do you enjoy your job?"

"Yes. And there is another dog here. He's a maverick."

Moose conveyed to me that the other dog didn't work as hard as he did.

When I mentioned the conversation to the ranchers, they exclaimed. "The other dog's name is Maverick!"

RABBIT REPRIMAND

Josh brought his rabbit to be read by the group at one of my workshops. I conversed with this female rabbit as part of a demonstration in animal communication. She told me a few things about Josh; then said, "Why does he give me that crappy lettuce?" She radiated indignation.

Josh said of his home–grown lettuce, "I didn't like the way it looked but I didn't want to throw it away, so I gave it to her."

"If it's not good enough for you, it's not good enough for me!" And she added, "And don't ever do that again!"

A sheepish look spread over his face. He said, "OK."

There are no secrets in the animal world.

CHAPTER TEN

A Talk with the Wild Side

"If you talk to the animals, they will talk with you, and you will know each other. If you do not talk to them, you will not know them; and what you do not know, you will fear. What one fears, one destroys."

~ Chief Dan George

ANTS AND SQUIRRELS?

Some creatures just don't work well with humans—like ants and squirrels. They don't feel a need to abide by our rules. They operate on pure instinct. Even the threat of extermination does not influence them. I have not discovered a motivator to offer in bargaining for a change in behavior in these two species.

On many occasions I have talked with ants about co-existing. I tried to persuade them to leave my home and stay in a particular area with the promise I would not disturb them. Their scornful attitude was, "We were here first." I tried to reach an agreement by offering them a plant for their own use if they would leave my other plants alone. They stubbornly refused to compromise. They are like marauding Vikings. They just take what they want.

Many clients have called me to complain about squirrels on their property. Sometimes they were concerned about the squirrels' safety, worried that their dogs would injure or kill them. Although I am able to communicate with the squirrels, I have had difficulty reaching any kind of compromise in their behavior. Wild squirrels hold an attitude like teenagers: "Don't tell me what to do. I will do what I want to do." They don't trust humans and they are very territorial. In addition, they have long memories and hold grudges.

Obviously, I still have a lot to learn from these species. I continue to look for solutions that will be acceptable to all parties.

I have had better luck with raccoons.

RESISTANT RACCOON

I was contacted to communicate with a raccoon that was holding up the renovation of a building to be used as a healing center for women. A mother raccoon and her three babies had taken up residence in an attic wall. The contractor managed to pick up the three babies and take them to a wildlife rehab center, but the mother remained elusive. She avoided the traps and continued to live in the attic.

Two options were offered. She could allow herself to be trapped unharmed and be reunited with her babies. Later, the entire family could be relocated to another wild area. The second option was to leave the house and never come back. I assured her that her babies would be well cared for until they were old enough to be released into the wild. If she remained in the building, she risked injury or death. She chose to leave.

Another intriguing part of this story was the presence of an angry and overbearing male earthbound spirit in the building. He had influenced the raccoon to stay there in an effort to hinder the renovator's work and deter the owner from her plans. He caused continual problems during the renovations because he hated women and did not want his former residence to become a healing center. Strange ongoing construction problems were confirmed by the new owner. Later in my career, I discovered a very powerful dowser who can remove such negative presences.

BABY BEARS AND A PUMA

One of my clients was licensed to board exotic animals until they could be placed into a permanent living situation. She called me when a brown bear cub and a black bear cub, both three months old, came into her care. Playing with the two was so much fun! They obviously enjoyed each other's company and the ranch provided them every amenity, including a swimming pool and a climbing tree. However, when I connected with them, they both expressed heartbreaking sorrow at the loss of their mothers.

At the same ranch, I communicated with a lovable ten–year–old puma, another rescued animal. The puma followed his human parents around like a pet dog. He told me he loved to ride around the ranch in the golf cart with his human dad. He also told me his favorite food was fresh raw chicken, a meal his human mom told me she provided on a regular basis.

HARRIED HORSE

A woman called me to determine the cause of her mare's agitation and injured leg. The vets had been treating the horse's swollen leg with no improvement. They could not diagnose the root cause of the injury.

During the phone session, I connected with the very agitated mare. I recognized her emotion as a state of fear.

"Why are you so fearful?" I wondered if she might be afraid of the vets or medical procedures.

She communicated extreme fear of a snake that had invaded her stall. The mare showed me an image of herself stomping around in the stall and the snake biting her.

To my surprise, the snake jumped into our conversation. She said she was only doing her job of keeping down the local population of rats and mice.

"The horse was trying to kill me. I was just protecting myself."

I stated my regret to both snake and horse that the situation was so traumatic for them.

An image of snake eggs under a cement overhang nearby appeared in my mind .

The mare's caretaker revealed she had found the snake eggs in the exact spot I described. She also told me that the vets had been treating the horse for a spider bite. The information from our phone session identified the true cause of the swollen leg, allowing the mare the correct remedy. The caretaker asked me to assure her mare that she would take precautions to prevent the snake's return.

GEORGE THE FISH

Until George, it never occurred to me that I could communicate with fish. Greta asked me to communicate with her friend, a Siamese fighting fish, to make sure he was happy. She was concerned about his welfare when he stayed in her office by himself on weekends. When I made contact, his response was immediate. He liked the location of his habitat in the office and was entertained by the frequent visits of humans who came to see Greta. He said the habitat itself was boring. A fishbowl with one little house on the bottom did not provide him with enough stimulation. I suggested to Greta that she add and rotate items to please George.

"Gosh. I never even thought about that," she told me.

She happily obliged her fish friend.

This short story tells us any species we choose as a pet needs some consideration for the enrichment of their environment.

FISH FAN

I enjoyed a wonderful visit at a client's gorgeous 10,000–acre Texas ranch populated with abundant wildlife. A clear freshwater creek flowed through the property and meandered around the main house. I wandered down to a dock on the creek to take in the spectacular view of the limestone cliffs that rose into the sky beyond the opposite bank. As I drank in the beauty and serenity of the moment, a multitude of fish caught my attention. The peacefulness of the fish, combined with the landscape, created a special energy that inspired me to meditate. As I settled into a meditative state, I connected with the consciousness of the fish. Calmness enveloped us. As I came to the end of the meditation, I thanked the fish for their wonderful contribution to this environment and the quiet energy they shared with me. When I opened my eyes, I discovered the fish had spread out fan–like in a half circle at the end of the pier with their heads facing me. In that moment, I realized that I had received an extraordinary gift of acknowledgment from the fish for my simple appreciation of their place in nature.

WILD AND FREE

The first communication I had with dolphins took place during a boat ride off Destin Beach in the Florida Panhandle. Our boat attracted a pod of dolphins who wanted to play near the boat's bow.

Eager to talk to dolphins, I said, "Tell me about yourselves."

One independent and rebellious male responded. I nicknamed him Spike.

He said the four females in his pod chose to be with him and could leave any time. He also said that dolphins swim upside down as a proposition for sex. "We enjoy our life of freedom."

"And, how do you feel about humans?"

He said he found humans mostly boring. We are too "serious." Our conversation didn't last long because he quickly lost interest.

AWKWARD OBSERVATION

Maureen volunteered for a dolphin rescue organization that worked to rehabilitate injured dolphins until they could be released into the wild. She was required to observe a male dolphin alone in a tank who was recovering from a near–death experience and take detailed notes of his behavior and overall well–being. He appeared to be healing. However, he developed a strange behavior. As he approached a rope near the surface of the water, he would flip himself on his back and scrape his belly under the rope. She called me because she feared that he may have developed any one of a number of problems—from a skin condition to a digestive malady—and this change in behavior could be his attempt to ease his discomfort.

When I connected with the dolphin, I started laughing. He clearly was feeling better as this was his way of stimulating himself sexually. When I told him he was upsetting Maureen, he let me know he appreciated her concern but he refused to stop because he was enjoying himself so much! Embarrassed and shocked, Maureen said, "OK, whatever, but I don't think I can put this in the notes!"

TWO CRICKETS AND A FROG WALK INTO A ROOM . . .

In this interesting occupation of mine, I never know who or what is going to show up. Jake, a journalist for an Internet publication, arranged to film me communicating with animals. He walked into the room holding a box and plopped into a chair in front of me. He then carefully removed the lid of the box to reveal two live crickets. One happily jumped around. The other cricket lay on its back with legs flailing in the air.

He asked, "Can you tell me what's wrong with this little guy?"

"Are these pets or food?"

"Both."

Despite the crickets' impending fate, I perceived that he provided good care for the crickets in the interim.

The flailing cricket showed me that Jake had a roommate who smoked a lot. The smoke made the cricket sick.

When I relayed this to Jake, a long silence followed.

Then he said, "Are you telling me that my cricket is stoned?"

Everyone in the room laughed.

I talked to the exotic frog next. Jake advised against touching the bright green and very delicate skin. The frog appeared well–maintained and traveled in a special portable frog habitat. The frog told me how much he liked Jake and Jake's really funny corny jokes. He said Jake's friends did not appreciate the jokes as much as he did. The cameraman laughed and interjected that Jake told corny jokes all the time.

CHAPTER ELEVEN

Are You Ready to Listen?

"Change the way you look at things and the things you look at will change."

~Wayne Dyer

REASONS FOR COMMUNICATION

Animals appreciate consultation regarding important matters. Please talk to your animal in advance about moving, euthanasia, and bringing another pet into the household. Other important discussions with your pet could include divorce, travel, boarding, health issues, behavior, food choices, and relationships with others (animals or humans) in the household. By discussing these topics we show our respect and concern for their desires and needs. Or you may want to improve your relationship by conducting frequent check–in chats.

RECEIVING INFORMATION

Everyone has some ability to communicate with animals. Each professional communicator has developed an effective personal method of connecting to animals. Discover your method by attending classes and seminars, and exploring different techniques. I have found that the guidance of an experienced and live instructor speeds up the learning process. Working with a group also allows you the opportunity to verify the information you receive. Allow yourself to make mistakes. Your skills can improve with practice.

Communicating with animals involves sending and receiving information intuitively. Animals will send information in words, pictures, colors, symbols, odors, emotions, or physical sensations. You may receive this information as a physical sensation in your body or as a mental impression. Information may have to be connected. For instance, a dog showed me wind, then rain, then fright. I deduced he was afraid of thunderstorms.

You may experience an entire story instantly, much like downloading data on a lightning–fast network. At a different level of consciousness, you retain a complete understanding of the story but you must translate it into everyday words. This is referred to as a "knowing" in psychic literature. Bringing this knowing into a translation can be complex. Sometimes, the information comes to you directly, and there is little or no need to translate it. Retaining flexibility is vital to adapt to the changing modes in the flow of information.

Remember, what you are actually receiving is an energy transmission, and your brain converts it into some kind of representation for your understanding.

Put aside any preconceived ideas. The more you practice communication, the more adept you become at recognizing other souls' efforts to communicate with you, whether they are living or deceased.

Personal judgments can also slow down the reception of information. A group of my students had difficulty reading a rabbit that had been brought in for a workshop. They had read each other's pets correctly earlier in the day, but this exercise had stumped them. Their judgments blocked them. The rabbit's owner had shared that he raised the rabbits for food. When the participants heard this, their own negative feelings regarding the fate of the rabbits prevented them from shifting into a receptive and neutral space.

One technique I often employ is to use a type of automatic writing. I jot down a word, phrase, or complete sentence for any thought that comes to me. I include as many details as possible.

Ashley sent me the following account after using this technique in one of my workshops on animal communication. It is an excellent description of a beginner's first communication attempt.

Jeanie and I were paired for the animal communication practice. I had never met Jeanie, nor did I get a chance to mingle with her before the session started. Jeanie and I exchanged pictures of our pooches and began the meditation. I had no idea what to expect. We were told to write down anything and everything that came to us, so that is what I did. Placing my hand on Jeanie's photo of her pet, I closed my eyes and held my breath. Then I realized that I really needed to breathe to be relaxed and open in order to communicate. Almost immediately, I relaxed and saw an apple. The apple was like a picture that you would see on an Etch A Sketch—the background was all black, and the apple was an outline of grey. The apple I saw in my mind's eye was complete with stem and leaf, something I thought was very interesting because, when I think of an apple, I don't normally think of a leaf on the apple.

I wrote down the apple with the stem and leaf, in case they were important details. I wasn't sure what you should ask a dog. I mentally asked her dog, Libby: "What's your favorite food? Do you like to play outside? What do you love to do?"

The pictures kept coming. Then I began to feel a little uncomfortable. My back felt stiff. I noticed pain in my shoulder. This was weird, because I don't normally have back pain. It happened so suddenly that, after a few minutes, I decided I should write down my pain also!

I kept concentrating. Pictures flew through my mind so fast I couldn't figure out what they meant. I had no idea if I was really communicating with Jeanie's pet, and this was frustrating. I could hear other people from the seminar writing on their papers, and I just knew they were having full-blown conversations with their animals.

Next, I saw the grey outline of a human. The person moved as if walking and wore a bright blue jacket of some sort. I knew it was a jacket because I saw a blob of blue shaped like a long–sleeved shirt, but there was a dark line down the center of it, like a zipper. I wrote down, "person with blue jacket."

The next thing I saw was the outline of a white bird, a very simple V–shape with flapping wings. The bird kept flying out of the picture. I wrote down, "white bird."

Jeanie confirmed the information I received. She and Libby visit her horses regularly. She feeds apples to the horses and Libby too. She added that she wears a blue zippered jacket when she goes out to check on the horses. Jeanie affirmed that Libby had shoulder pain. After the reading, my pain disappeared.

At first, the white bird I saw meant nothing to Jeanie. However, later she remembered a traumatic experience involving a white turkey.

INITIATING CONTACT

Every communicator must establish a way of preparing and protecting themselves before they open up energetically. The communicator should exclude harmful energies from the invitation to connect. Clearing residual negative energies after a communication is also important in that not only does it clear the body, it completely severs the connection. Leaving that connection open can deplete your energy.

I find the following practices helpful in my work. I encourage you to explore different techniques to discover what works best for you.

PHYSICAL PREPARATION

Run, jog, or jump outside for a minimum of five minutes. In Chinese philosophy, this is a method to connect with the energy between Heaven and Earth. The motion activates energy in your body. Vigorous exercise releases stress and prepares your body for meditation.

Additionally, at least a ten–minute yoga session will also stretch your mental and physical muscles. I encourage you to explore yoga poses that specifically open intuition.

MEDITATION

The practice of meditation strengthens intuitive senses. Meditate at least fifteen minutes every day. If you start and end the day with a short meditation with eyes closed, the discipline will train your mind to withstand emotional fluctuations and help you to sleep better at night. Meditation empties our minds, effectively turns off the "brain chatter," and permits quiet space for the intuitive information to enter our consciousness. It balances the left and right hemispheres of our brain. Most of us allow the left side of the brain to dominate our thinking. This side is used for reasoning, learning, language, and mathematics.

The right side of the brain is used for creativity, inspiration, and intuition.

A grounding meditation is essential for opening up your intuitive ability. This specific meditation pulls the energy from your head into your central body and down through the soles of your feet, until you are linked with the center of earth. It allows you to be energized and fully present in the "now" moment. Afterward, you will not have the dreamy or spacey feeling that you might get with some other forms of meditation. You will be calm, clear, and receptive. You are then connected with the same energy that animals engage automatically in their natural state.

SUGGESTIONS FOR A SUCCESSFUL COMMUNICATION

It's easier to begin your practice sessions with pets of friends or neighbors. The emotion you feel for your own pet can distort the results. In addition, intimate knowledge presents difficulty in verification. The following suggestions prepare you for a successful session.

1. Write out your intentions or questions. This will help you stay organized and obtain maximum information.

2. When you are ready to begin, choose a time when the household is calm and you have no distractions. You do not need to restrict the animal. Usually, animals enjoy the energy connection and may become very relaxed during the session. Sometimes animals fall asleep

during communication. This does not affect the quality of the information.

3. Calm yourself and clear your mind with a grounding meditation. Envision yourself enveloped within a protective shield or bubble before you open your energies to the surrounding field. This step is imperative to obtain an accurate reading, because strong emotion and left–brain chatter can interfere with clear reception.

4. Request guidance from a higher source or multiple sources. You may ask God, Universal Intelligence, Expert Animal Communication Angels, Guides, or the source to which you feel the greatest connection. Your request may be in the form of a prayer if you desire. Ask for assistance in receiving only information that is for the highest good. State your intentions—whether to resolve a problem, request or relay information, or just to chat with the animal.

5. If you don't have the actual animal nearby, you may look at a picture or visualize the animal. When you enter into the universal field through a quiet meditative state, physical proximity to the animal is not required, as you can

energetically connect to the animal within the field.

6. Always address animals with respect and by name, if possible. A wild or unnamed animal may be addressed as Mr. or Ms., which will show them your respect.

7. Be open to any information you may receive. Most likely, it will differ from your expectations. Develop good listening skills. Don't use baby talk, as it will offend some animals. If they get bored or refuse to talk, thank them and attempt another session later. Sometimes, if you're giving them information, they will listen and understand but won't necessarily respond. Just accept this preferred method of communication. Also, don't expect too much too soon, especially with your own pets. They are accustomed to hearing your voice so they may not respond to your new–found skill immediately. To us, this is like playing with a new toy, but the animal may be bored with all our questions or comments. It is best to limit the session time in the beginning.

8. To overcome frustration in my early attempts to communicate with my dog

Trina, I discovered a method to get her attention. She had become accustomed to responding only to the sound of my voice and she ignored my mental commands. I visualized myself walking to the kitchen and pulling her favorite treat out of the jar. Then I visualized walking to her location and handing her the treat. When I opened my eyes, Trina was staring at me and salivating. That was my verification that she received my mental message. Of course, I followed through by actually giving her the treat.

9. If you are talking with an animal for the first time, try to get a sense of the animal's personality. Ask it to tell you about itself, things it likes, or ask it to share its opinions. In this way, you again show respect and thereby open a line of communication.

10. Establish trust. When you sense the animal is comfortable with you, ask your questions and relay your information. Give them an opportunity to do the same.

11. If it is not your pet, do not ask about health problems without permission from the caretaker. If the information is volunteered, acknowledge it. Keep in

mind, your topics should be appropriate, and sensitive information should remain confidential. Use discretion in sharing the information you receive. Some of the information, such as the presence of cancer or other serious conditions, may be difficult to pass on to the caretaker. Avoid serious subjects until you have gained significant and verifiable experience in your communication.

12. When you receive something you don't understand, note it anyway. The information may seem mundane or unimportant, but it could be an important clue. That clue could be a segment of a string of information.

13. Thank the animal when you are ready to end the session. And don't forget to thank your higher sources for their assistance and guidance.

CLEARING ENERGY

At this point, and this is the most important step, clear your body of harmful energy. Inevitably, you will take on some unwanted energy from the connection that may manifest as an illness in your mind or body at a later date. An effective technique I employ is jumping in place or jogging for three to five minutes. I throw my arms to the ground continually as I am jumping to throw the harmful energy into the ground. I state my intention that Mother Earth take the energy, cleanse it, and then reuse it for good.

I continue by visualizing a portable vacuum to extract any residual negativity. Then I end by mentally polishing and repairing any tears or smudges in my aura with a soft clean cloth. This is a variation of a technique I learned from noted psychic James Van Praagh.

ANIMAL COMMUNICATION STYLES

Animals' communication styles reflect individual personalities and opinions. Like humans, animals' personalities vary. They may be humorous and fun or dignified and proper, and some will startle you with obscene language. You might be surprised to find that some animals lie.

For instance, Dino, a tricky little dachshund mix, interrupted me, as I was about to negotiate a change in his undesirable behavior.

"I was a penguin in a previous life!"

I knew it wasn't true, but I relayed his remark to my client.

Excited by this bit of information, she replied, "I think it's true! He always wants to get in the hot tub with us."

At that moment I received an intuitive flash that the two of them had enjoyed a TV documentary a few days ago about penguins. When she verified this, I knew the cagey dog wanted extra attention and was trying to impress her. Even after we identified the source of his allegation, my client preferred to believe he had really been a penguin. What a character!

My favorite part of communication is discovering an animal's personality. It brings to mind that famous Forrest Gump line, "Life is like a box of chocolates, you never know what you are going to get."

CHAPTER TWELVE

Who is the Higher Species?

"Knowing others is wisdom; knowing the self is enlightenment."

~ *Tao Te Ching*

When I initially became aware of my animal communication abilities, I thought helping animals was my soul's purpose. As I gained more experience, I noticed that animals were giving me spiritual, physical, and emotional information for their humans. Glimpses of key concepts about the big picture permeated my consciousness.

Most people accept information from their pets more readily than from any human. Animals choose to come into this life to assist us with our spiritual lessons as well as to work on their own soul progression. They reflect our illnesses, our emotions, and the consequences of our actions and non–actions. They teach us patience, understanding, respect, loyalty, and unconditional love—except for cats. They can have lots of conditions!

I found truth in the statement, "The teacher is the student, and the student is the teacher." As my career progressed, the animals and I visibly touched each other's lives. An animal frequently assumes the role of teacher.

BORDER COLLIE LESSON

A man skeptical of animal communication, but desperate to determine the origination of issues with a particular horse, called me for help. During a conference call with him, I was able to furnish him with verifiable information related to his horse's medical problem.

The man's wife listened and, when I finished with the horse, said, "When we bought this horse, a dog came with it—a border collie. Can you talk with the border collie?"

Their twelve–year–old son wanted to know why the dog wouldn't chase the ball when he threw it.

I found the dog to be very bright and full of energy. She told me she refused to chase the ball because the boy called her stupid. He immediately denied this, but his mother verified it.

This simple piece of information made the family aware of the intelligence and sensitivity of the dog. Once alerted, they had the option to alter their attitude and the way they interacted with their animals.

At a much later time, an outside source, who knew this man and his family well, contacted me to thank me for the reading. This source shared with me a concern regarding methods the man had previously employed in training the horse. As a result of the reading, the man softened his treatment of animals.

SLITHERY STUFF

Synchronicity continues to play a major role in my spiritual development. One occurrence happened during a communication workshop I attended years ago. The facilitator led us through a meditation to overcome fears of certain types of animals. A vision of a large yellow boa constrictor, the creature that I most feared, appeared in the meditation and coiled up in a large heap in my lap. It seemed very real. Although I tried to show appreciation for its presence, I could not imagine myself touching it. Later, I felt regret that I missed that opportunity.

The next day I met a young couple in my apartment complex. I was stunned to see them holding and petting the same snake from my meditation! I gathered my courage and asked the couple's permission to pet the snake. They encouraged me to stroke their pet and told me how much they adored her while she hung over the shoulders of the young man. I'm still not completely comfortable with snakes but I now have a much better understanding of their consciousness.

I met another beautiful and large yellow boa in a pet store some time later. They called her Sophie. She lived in a huge open crate in the center of the room as a permanent resident. During our brief encounter, she expressed distress regarding the fear she felt coming from so many people who visited. This time I could set my fear aside and empathize with the snake.

CAT–ALYSTS FOR PERSONAL GROWTH

Lucy, a cat lover extraordinaire, discovered me when her rescued Black Smoke Persian, Ashley, continued to urinate on her bed. Lucy had tried all the conventional methods to stop the inappropriate behavior with no success.

She opted for an offbeat approach by reaching out to me. She had no experience with animal communicators and had expressed her doubts about the existence of authentic psychic abilities. But she was a desperate skeptic, so she decided to hire me to visit her home, read all of her pets, and troubleshoot Ashley's problem.

The second strong motivation for contacting me was to connect with a much beloved companion, Midnight, who had died two months earlier after a brief, unexpected illness. Midnight's passing had left Lucy with an ache in her heart that was not healed by the presence of her other cats.

Midnight told me she had been delighted by the upbeat, "musica Latina" that Lucy played and danced to in the house. She said Lucy would hold Midnight on one of her shoulders as they moved together to the rhythm. Midnight told me it brought happy energy to the home.

Lucy sobbed during the reading as I relayed more details from Midnight.

When her second Persian, Annabelle, died unexpectedly months later, Lucy called me again. She was disturbed because Annabelle died from complications resulting from a routine dental cleaning and extraction performed at a veterinarian's office.

She said, "The grief this time was as if a searing, hot sword had pierced through my soul, severing it irreparably. The occurrence of this senseless tragedy exactly five months after Midnight's death seemed too cruel a burden to endure."

In Lucy's anger, she had ordered a necropsy report from a major veterinarian college, and the report's result read "inconclusive." She considered filing a lawsuit against the offending vet for suspected malpractice. While she researched the details for a lawsuit, she started a blog to vent her anger and warn others about hidden dangers to pets, such as unsound veterinary practices and unwholesome commercial pet foods. She wanted to obtain some kind of justice for Annabelle through the blog, because she did not trust the legal system. Grief turned her into an activist overnight. Now, she wanted to know the truth of Annabelle's passing and what the cat had to say about a possible lawsuit.

During the reading, Annabelle conveyed her deep love for Lucy and encouraged her to seek a new more positive path and embrace changes that would lead her to help others in unexpected ways. Retribution was not the highest path for Lucy to follow. Annabelle advised that a lawsuit would be unsuccessful and Lucy should abandon the idea. Midnight joined the conversation and echoed Annabelle's comments. At that point, Lucy was able to surrender any residual negativity and turn her energy to seeking out new, positive directions.

She told me, "Since that reading, I've experienced great serenity as I feel that all is well in the spirit world with my pets. Our loving bonds still exist and empower me to move forward."

This is a note I received from Lucy sometime later:

> Since Midnight and Annabelle both passed on, their deaths opened up my mind to seeking enlightenment outside of the typical venues in which I'd sought answers to life's stresses and problems.

Formerly, I'd sought answers in mainstream religion, westernized medicine, and in other conventional offerings. Through my life's struggles and losses, I realized those institutions no longer served me.

Lucy now practices meditation and is getting involved in energy healing. She recently attended one of my workshops and was surprised to discover she could communicate with animals.

She said, "I approached the workshop with an open mind and I was inspired and touched by what I experienced and learned that day. I found I have a rudimentary skill in communicating with animals, and I was greatly surprised to tap into this part of myself. Myra claims we can all communicate with animals, but until it happened to me at the workshop, I remained skeptical that I could do it. I still practice the basic skills I learned, and sometimes it is easy for me to connect with a new animal or even a wild animal, but it will always be a work in progress for me. I gained many blessings by simply opening my mind to the possibilities of finding answers and fulfillment in new areas. Stepping out of my comfort zone and taking a few steps in new directions have greatly empowered me, and I continue to meet inspiring fellow travelers on similar paths."

Lucy's story is a perfect example of how communicating with animals can move us toward spiritual expansion.

A HEAD START

I met Laura when I gave animal communication lessons to a small, private group. At the conclusion of the seminar, I conducted mini–readings for the attendees. Laura handed me a photo of Troy, a black standard poodle.

Troy connected quickly and easily. He readily relayed details about Laura's personality and habits, including the organized way she kept her closets. She was meticulous about planning her wardrobe and accessory choices in advance. He expressed his admiration for her. Laura appeared slightly uncomfortable with the personal nature of the information Troy shared. I continued anyway, because I sensed an urgency about the communication.

The next piece of information scared me. Troy told me he was worried about Laura's brain. Laura thought that I was mistaken because she suffered from chronic heart problems. She shared that she had sustained two heart attacks.

I said, "He's not worried about your heart. Troy is worried about your aneurysm."

Laura maintained that Troy must be confused. She had a heart issue, not a brain aneurysm.

A very dynamic and busy professional, she did not think much more about the reading until a couple of years later. Her eyelid fluttered strangely. Troy's warning combined with her health history, persuaded her to call her cardiologist. He ultimately ordered a CAT scan of her body, and the results indicated an aneurysm in her brain. The doctors were able to surgically treat the aneurysm before it caused any further problems. Troy passed soon after Laura's surgery. He stayed with her as long as he could to offer support, his parting gift to her after a faithful and rewarding relationship.

I felt anxiety at the time Troy told me about the aneurysm because I didn't get any feedback on the accuracy of this reading. Two years later, I began to receive a lot of referrals from Laura. When people called for appointments, they told me about the aneurysm and Laura's brain surgery. I realized that Troy's information was accurate. This news relieved my mixed feelings regarding my interpretation of Troy's warning and, at the same time, my desire for Laura to not have a serious problem.

This experience taught me that everything happens in its own time, and not necessarily according to my expectations. It also reaffirmed to me animals have the ability to read our energy and what is happening in our bodies.

SOMETHING TO THINK ABOUT

Animals hold considerable wisdom that can be shared with us. They are naturally plugged into harmonious creation. Their sphere of perception extends way beyond ours in many ways. They have come into this life to help us and teach us. When I'm in that shared space with them, I experience clarity without judgment. They contribute to my continually expanding awe of the grand design of the universe.

These are highly evolved souls existing in animal bodies. Because many people don't acknowledge that animals have souls, they exhibit a lack of respect for these wonderful beings. I sometimes wonder, "Who is the higher species?"

CHAPTER THIRTEEN

An Awesome Ending

"It (the Cheshire cat) vanished quite slowly, beginning with the end of the tail, and ending with the grin, which remained some time after the rest of it had gone."

~ *Lewis Carroll*

PUTTING ALL THE CHIPS ON THE TABLE

When I first began experiencing success in animal communication, my friend Dr. Babbish suggested that I conduct sessions with her colleagues and their staff at a local veterinary clinic. We could arrange an afternoon when they could have a private session with a pet they brought in to work.

As she described this plan, I felt my body lock up with fear.

"Happy, I can't do that!"

"Why not?"

"What if I screw up and ruin your reputation?"

"Myra, I know you can do this. If you don't try, you'll never know for sure."

I realized she was right. I had to take the risk. So, we made the arrangements. I felt terror and apprehension the day I went to the clinic. But, as soon as I started the sessions, the fascinating information coming forward and the animals' personalities captured my total attention.

At the end of the day, I was exhausted and elated, because I had helped so many people make a connection with their animal friends. The entire experience exhilarated me as if I had stepped into a new world.

As my practice grew, my confidence increased concerning the entire animal communication experience. My relationship with the universe expanded. My spirituality deepened.

Along the way, I identified and addressed personal stumbling blocks. When I encountered new phenomena, I learned to go inside myself and look for guidance. With time, effort, and lots of practice, I discovered how to recognize and implement that guidance.

When people tell me I have a wonderful gift, I respond that the information comes from a higher source. I am simply the conduit or messenger. Learning to trust the information coming through has been a long process and has not always been easy. I learned to forgive myself for making mistakes. Dropping judgments and maintaining patience are still major challenges.

The importance of setting boundaries for self protection became imperative as my career progressed. Sometimes I received a warning not to do a particular reading. I ignored these warnings in the beginning. Eventually, I recognized their value. Some things must be learned the hard way from authentic experience.

Taking action with each new puzzle piece advances my spiritual development. The more I develop myself, the more I can pass on beneficial information to clients. And, as I observe the sometimes life–altering material that comes through, I am encouraged to extend the expansion of my awareness.

A FRENCH BULLDOG LOVE STORY

Jacques demonstrated that animals serve a higher purpose in the blueprint of human affairs. This cute French bulldog's skin erupted in painful bleeding sores, despite his family's best efforts to remedy stubborn skin problems with expensive prescribed medications. The family sent Jacques to my friend and top–notch animal nutritionist healer/trainer, Caron, when steroids wouldn't control the problem. Caron hoped that a change of environment and a new diet would heal the dog. In spite of her best efforts, the dog's skin continued to erupt. She was well–aware of the energy connection between animals and their caretakers. She suspected some kind of trauma must have happened in his household.

After questioning the family, Caron discovered Jacques' main caretaker and lifelong friend was a teenage girl. Molly resided at a private drug rehabilitation facility hundreds of miles from her home. This was a last–resort decision after the family had tried other, sometimes extreme, methods to help her. A conference call was arranged with Molly, her mother, her therapist, Caron, Jacques, and myself.

Jacques asked me to tell Molly, "Remember the balloon—it was exciting."

Molly responded that she would inhale nitrous oxide from a balloon at home in her bedroom. It would give her the giggles until she started to pass out. Jacques would charge and bark at the balloon, which caused Molly to stop because she thought it scared him. He told me he wasn't scared but he thought it was weird when her voice changed.

Jacques continued by showing me Molly's clothes.

"What is with the clothes?" I wondered aloud.

Molly laughed and said she dressed him up in her clothes when she was younger. He really liked that.

I added, "Jacques keeps telling me he loves frogs."

Molly and her mom exclaimed together, "Oh!"

Molly added, "He loves to eat them. We can always tell when he's dined on a frog when he's been outside, because he returns with a foaming mouth."

Jacques was reflecting Molly's energy. As she was addicted to drugs, he was addicted to toxic frogs. I told her, "As you get better, he is going to get better too. "

The call continued for a long time. Molly dealt with a lot of guilt regarding Jacques. She had left him for hours in the car when she would go to see drug dealers. Although she had been able to forgive herself through therapy, she couldn't get past letting her little dog down. She kept asking me if Jacques forgave her.

He told me he was never angry with her. He had been worried about her well-being when she was out of his sight because he couldn't protect her. Then Jacques described the facility where she was staying, so she would know that he was always connected to her.

At this point, I explained that this connection accelerated the symptoms Jacques experienced. When the drug toxins were leaving Molly's body, Jacques experienced this as skin trauma.

Molly's love for Jacques proved to be a major motivation for her healing. He had been her constant companion for eleven of her sixteen years. She gradually earned higher allowance levels at the facility until she could leave for short outings. Her parents would bring Jacques with them on visits.

A team effort contributed to Molly's rehabilitation. Caron's knowledge of the family, and her observation that Molly and Jacques regressed at about the same time, tipped her off to their strong energetic connection. Molly's supportive family and therapist laid the groundwork for her recovery. The communication between Jacques and Molly allowed her to understand Jacques' viewpoint and alleviate her guilt, the final piece that held her back. But mostly, Molly's love for her little French bulldog provided the inspiration that gave her the strength to recover from her addiction.

Because of Jacques's love and support, Molly chose to continue the rehab program at the facility until she graduated from school. Molly progressed so impressively that, months later, I heard the facility and the therapist were considering using animal communication in their rehab treatment program. Molly had advanced several levels within days of the telephone conference. The average progression and healing take months.

AWESOME AND THE GIRL WITH THE PINK SHOES

A horse trainer had encouraged the Maxwells to consult with me regarding one of their Arabian horses. They were trying to determine the origin of the horse's problems.

As I arrived at their barn, I met three people with hands on hips.

They said, "We're skeptical about this animal communication stuff, but we heard you're good."

Their attitude didn't bother me, because I had learned to just go to work, doing what I do, and let the rest happen. They had intended for me to talk with only one horse but they were so pleased with the results of the first horse's communication, they asked me to talk to all their horses.

I worked my way down the stalls to the sixth, and last, horse, Awesome.

"What information do you want from this horse?" I asked to expedite things, as it was getting late.

"We just want to know if there is anyone in particular he prefers?"

Awesome described a little girl with long blond hair. He commented on how much he enjoyed her company and described the bond they shared.

I asked the Maxwells if they knew the girl he described. They explained the horse was up for sale and several people had looked at him. They described a family that had brought their young blonde daughter to ride Awesome. It was obvious to everyone the two enjoyed each other's company.

Then Awesome showed me the girl's pink shoes. When I asked the Maxwells if they had noticed her pink shoes, they maintained she had worn cowboy boots on both occasions. Perplexed, I questioned the horse about the pink shoes, but Awesome adamantly insisted the girl wore pink shoes.

I asked the Maxwells if they would call the couple to see if their daughter owned a pair of pink shoes. I received my answer a few days later.

Mrs. Maxwell called me and said, "Myra, you're not going to believe this! The little girl's parents told me that she prefers to wear her favorite pair of gaudy pink shoes almost everywhere she goes."

While they were discussing the mystery of how the horse could have known about the pink shoes, their daughter interrupted the conversation and said, "Mama, every night I ride that horse in my dreams, and I'm always wearing my pink shoes."

The implications of her dreams still give me goosebumps. Obviously, an association exists between species that transcends our ideas of reality. How did the horse know about the pink shoes? Was he able to "see" her nighttime dreams when she rode him, or did he maintain a telepathic connection with her? On further introspection, I realized they had been meeting in a spiritual dimension. This additional insight raises many more questions.

What are these spiritual dimensions? How can the animals tap so easily into these worlds while it takes most of us years of training and experience to catch a small glimpse of them? What does this indicate for the future of mankind?

As my career has opened me up to greater information and other dimensions, so it may be for other humans who are just beginning to peer beyond their day–to–day experiences. I don't pretend I understand it all, but I'm excited by the vision of the great potential of our future. Who knows where all this information is leading us?

Animal communication is teaching us that we are more than what visibly lies on the surface.

I now understand that the Earth and her inhabitants are truly interconnected spirits. We are a part of a well–orchestrated symphony that helps us evolve to a higher understanding of the universe and clarifies the road to better choices for who we decide to be. I am delighted to be part of this awesome story.

58605830R00081

Made in the USA
Lexington, KY
14 December 2016